LISP
AN INTERACTIVE APPROACH

OTHER BOOKS OF INTEREST
FROM COMPUTER SCIENCE PRESS

Lowell A. Carmony, Robert J. McGlinn, Ann Miller Millman, and
Jerry P. Becker
Apple Pascal: A Self-Study Guide for the Apple II Plus, IIe, and IIc
Problem Solving in Apple Pascal

Lowell A. Carmony and Robert L. Holliday
Macintosh™ Pascal

William Findlay and David Watt
Pascal: An Introduction to Methodical Programming, Second Edition

Donald J. Geenen
Learning Apple® FORTRAN

Narain Gehani
Advanced C: Food for the Educated Palette
C: An Advanced Introduction
C for Personal Computers: IBM, PC, AT&T PC 6300, and Compatibles

Rachelle S. Heller, C. Dianne Martin, and June L. Wright
LOGOWORLDS

Ellis Horowitz, Editor
Programming Languages: A Grand Tour, Second Edition

W. Douglas Maurer
Apple* Assembly Language
Commodore 64™ Assembly Language: A Course of Study Based on the
  DEVELOP-64 Assembler/Editor/Debugger

Vern A. McDermott, Andrew J. Young, and Diana M. Fisher
Learning Pascal Step by Step

James J. McGregor and Alan H. Watt
Simple Pascal

Ronald H. Perrott and Donald C. S. Allison
Pascal for FORTRAN Programmers

Kurt James Schmucker
Fuzzy Sets, Natural Language Computations, and Risk Analysis

*Apple is a trademark of Apple Computers, Inc.

LISP
AN INTERACTIVE APPROACH

STUART C. SHAPIRO

*State University of New York
at Buffalo*

COMPUTER SCIENCE PRESS

To Caren

Computer Science Press
1803 Research Boulevard
Rockville, Maryland 20850
1 2 3 4 5 6 Printing   Year 90 89 88 87 86

Library of Congress Cataloging-in-Publication Data

Shapiro, Stuart Charles.
  LISP : an interactive approach.

  Includes index.
  1. LISP (Computer program language)   I. Title.
QA76.73.L23S53   1986   005.13′3   85-24324
ISBN 0-88175-069-7

CONTENTS

Preface

The purpose of this book is to teach the LISP programming language. The book is intended to be a self-paced study guide, requiring supplements from an instructor, manual, consultant, or friend only to fill in the details of the local operating system and LISP dialect. It has been used, through growth and revision, at the State University of New York at Buffalo since 1978, as the text of the LISP portion of Data Structures and Programming Languages courses, as a self-study guide for students deficient in LISP at the beginning of an Artificial Intelligence course, and as a self-study guide for students and faculty members learning LISP independently. It has also been used at Oregon State University, Simon Fraser University, Canisius College, State University of New York College at Fredonia, and Erie Community College. It has received excellent reviews from its users.

LISP is the language of choice for work in Artificial Intelligence and in Symbolic Algebra. It is also important in the study of Programming Languages, because, since its inception over twenty-five years ago, it has had full recursion, the conditional expression, the equivalence of program and data structure, its own evaluator available to the programmer, and extensibility—the syntactic indistinguishability of programmer-defined functions and "built-in" operators. It is also the paradigm of "functional" or "applicative" programming. Because of the varied interests in LISP, I have tried to present it in a general and neutral setting, rather than specifically in the context of any of the special fields in which it is used.

Above all, LISP is an *interactive* language. A LISP program is not built up from imperative statements, but from *expressions*, each of which has a *value*. The LISP programmer sits in front of a terminal, interacting with the LISP evaluator. During such a session, a program gets written, read, tested, modified, and saved for future use. Most LISP implementations provide more than just a programming language; they provide an entire environment including tracing and "break" packages, editors, filers, compilers, and other programmer aids, almost all written in LISP itself. The modus operandi of users of batch-oriented languages such as FORTRAN, ALGOL, COBOL, PL/I, Pascal, and SNOBOL is alien to the LISP programmer. I, myself, have never punched a LISP S-expression on a card in over twenty years of LISP programming.

It therefore bothered me that no LISP text taught LISP in a way specially designed for its interactive nature. In fact, until recently, there were very few LISP texts at all. I learned LISP by experimenting with it, typing S-expressions into a terminal and seeing what happened. I have recommended this method to others, and was finally motivated enough to prepare this guide for my students. Their reaction and that of my colleagues encouraged me to keep extending the guide into a full book.

Teaching LISP by having the student sit down at a terminal and experiment right from the start influences the order of topics. For peace of mind, the first thing a novice needs to know about being in a new environment is how to get out. Therefore, Chapter 1 is concerned solely with getting into LISP and getting back out. A novice makes mistakes (so do we all). Therefore, it is important to show the break package environment and error messages early. Since typing errors will occur, backspace and delete keys are important, and the student needs to experience the entire character set. The general approach here is to prepare the student for the unexpected. Since new concepts must be built on existing conceptual structures, numeric examples are used before symbolic examples. The LISP editor is introduced when I think the student must be getting sick of retyping an entire function definition to correct an error.

Since the best language for defining LISP is LISP itself, most LISP functions are introduced by having the student define them first. This means that some functions I have been tempted to discuss early have been put off until the student has enough background to define them.

I have tried to write the exercises so that it is reasonable to expect the student to do all of them. Therefore, the only long projects are distributed through the text as small exercises modifying and extending functions that are saved on a file.

Like every language that has existed for some time, LISP has developed dialects. This is especially easy for LISP since its extensibility allows every LISP programmer to be a systems programmer as well. Good ideas get popular locally and develop into a dialect. Good implementations of LISP get passed around to other sites and local dialects become widespread. Good ideas also spread by word of mouth and get incorporated into different dialects in slightly different ways. All this creates difficulties for the textbook author who wants his book to be useful for users of different dialects. My problem is even worse, since features that make life easy or difficult for the interactive user, such as character and line erase keys, interrupt keys, and system control commands, are dependent on the local computer system and even on the terminal being used.

What I have tried to do to allow for dialect and system differences is the following. As much as possible, I have tried to limit the discussion to features common to all LISPs, leaving dialect-dependent features for advanced study. Where features are discussed that vary across dialects and systems, I discuss several variations, mentioning specific dialects where I can, and advise the student to check with his or her manual or with his or her actual system by experimenting. In my role as teacher (indirectly via the text), if I cannot provide specific information, I can at least tell the student what information is needed when. It is up to the users of this text to judge how well I have succeeded. Naturally, I will appreciate being notified of variations I should have mentioned as well as of outright errors.

No one's ideas or approaches spring up in a vacuum. I am grateful to John McCarthy, who invented LISP; to Danny Bobrow and Mike Levin, who first taught me LISP; to all the authors of previous LISP books, including Clark Weissman, Dan Friedman, Laurent Siklossy, John R. Allen, Patrick Winston, Berthold Horn, Jim Meehan, Bob Wilensky, and David Touretzky; to my past and present colleagues who influenced my programming style, including Dan Friedman, Dave Wise, Mitch Wand, John Lowrance, Don McKay, Rich Fritzson, Joao Martins, and Ernesto Morgado; to Patricia Eberlein, John Case, Bill Rapaport, Brian Funt, and, especially, Bill Bregar for their comments after using drafts in their classes; to Jeff Ullman for his comments after reviewing a draft; and to Guy Steele for his very valuable suggestions and comments on two of the drafts. Of course, none of these people necessarily endorse this approach, nor are they responsible for any defects or errors. I am extremely grateful to Janet Root, Delores Dunston, and Bruce Bernstein for typing many of the revisions this manuscript has gone through; to Elizabeth Mergner, of Computer Science Press, who has exhibited a much-appreciated balance of patience and reminding; and, of course, to my wife Caren for her support, and for refraining from taking me on errands during the final push to finish this book.

To the Reader

The purpose of this book is to help you learn the programming language LISP (LISt Processing language) by experimenting with it via an interactive computer terminal. The recommended method is to read a section or two, sit down at a terminal and try the examples and exercises of those sections, leave the terminal and go on to the next sections, etc. It is important for you to do every exercise completely!

Unlike other programming languages, LISP does not operate on a series of imperative statements—"do this, then do this, etc.," but on expressions, called symbolic expressions or S-expressions, which LISP evaluates. A session with LISP involves typing in an S-expression; LISP evaluates it and prints the value; you then type in another S-expression; etc. Some S-expressions cause, as side-effects, new functions to be defined. These can then be used in other S-expressions. This is how complicated programs are written in LISP.

Don't worry about making mistakes. That's part of learning. If one of your S-expressions causes an error, try to figure out what it was and then continue on. Use the personalized manual on pages 139–143 to record features of your LISP system and use it for reference.

References

There are quite a few dialects of LISP. Some of these are mentioned explicitly, some aren't. Since all details of all dialects cannot be discussed, your own LISP manual is a necessary reference. The manuals I have relied on most in writing this book are:

1. J. K. Foderaro and K. L. Sklower. The FRANZ LISP Manual. Berkeley, CA: Regents of the University of California, 1980.

2. K. Konolige. *ALISP User's Manual*. Amherst, MA: University Computing Center, University of Massachusetts, 1977.

3. J. R. Meehan. *The New UCI LISP Manual*. Hillsdale, NJ: Lawrence Erlbaum, 1979.

4. K. M. Pitman. *The Revised MACLISP Manual*. MIT/LCS/TR-295, Cambridge, MA: Laboratory for Computer Science, MIT, 1983.

5. G. L. Steele, Jr. *COMMON LISP: THE LANGUAGE*. Maynard, MA: Digital Press, 1984.

6. W. Teitelman. *INTERLISP Reference Manual*. Palo Alto, CA: XEROX Palo Alto Research Centers, 1974.

7. D. Weinreb and D. Moon. *Lisp Machine Manual*. Cambridge, MA: MIT, 1981.

8. R. Wilensky. *LISPcraft*. New York: W. W. Norton, 1984.

Chapter 1

The Basics

1.1 Getting Started

Your goal for this section is to learn how to access your LISP and how to exit from it. Although this may not seem like much, it is obviously very important. It is also very dependent on the particular system you are using, so you will have to get much of the information from a manual, a teacher, or a friend.

The first problem is to *log onto* your computer system. This might simply involve turning on your microcomputer or it might require typing in some accounting information.

If you are using a LISP machine or have "booted" a microcomputer with a LISP disk, you will be already talking to LISP. Otherwise, you will have to access LISP. This might just require typing "lisp" or "LISP" (without the quotes) or it might first require retrieving the LISP system.

Once you are in LISP, most LISPs will tell you they are waiting for input by printing a *prompt*. This can be a question mark, an arrow, a colon, or something else. You are now supposed to type something to LISP called a *symbolic expression*, or an *S-expression*. We will get into great detail about what an S-expression is, but for now, let's use small integers, like 3.

When you type an S-expression to LISP (remember to end each entry by pressing the carriage return key), LISP will print the *value* of the S-expression, and then a new prompt. That's all there is to using LISP— you give it an S-expression, it gives you its value. Since the value of an integer is the integer itself, all LISP will do at this stage is echo your input.

On some LISPs, when you make a mistake, or when you make certain mistakes, LISP will enter its *break package*. The break package is just like normal LISP except information relevant to figuring out your error is available. We will look at this in more detail in later sections. For now, you just need to be able to recognize the break package and to know how to get out of it. We refer to normal LISP as *the top level* and to the break package as a *lower level*. If you make an error while in the break package, you will get into an even lower-level break package. You need to know how to get all the way back to the top level again.

The break package is recognizable because it uses a different prompt. For example, ALISP's top-level prompt is "?", while its break package prompt is "*". Franz LISP's top-level prompt is "->", its first-level break prompt is "<1>", its second-level break prompt is "<2>", and so on. To get out of ALISP's break package, we type (RETURN NIL). (The parentheses are vital.) To get out of Franz LISP's break package, we type ^D (which means press the "D" key while holding down the CONTROL or CNTRL key—the SHIFT key is not necessary) or (reset) (with the parentheses). (Note that some LISPs like capital letters, while others like small letters. Some don't care.) If you are several levels down in break packages, you may have to do this repeatedly.

If the LISP we're using has a break package, we can often force our way into it by typing the appropriate *interrupt key*. This may be the BREAK, RUB, or DEL key, or it may be some control character such as ^C. Sometimes, for the interrupt key to work, it must be struck before any other character is typed on the line, and sometimes it must be typed more than once in succession.

Back on top-level LISP, it's time to get off. To leave ALISP or UCI LISP, type (EXIT), parentheses included. To exit Franz LISP, type ^D or (exit). MACLISP uses (QUIT), INTERLISP uses (LOGOUT), others use (STOP), or even just STOP. Yours might be something else.

Finally, you need to know how to *log off* your computing system.

Exercises

1. What is the procedure for getting into your LISP? Write it here:

_____

_____

_____

2. What is the procedure for getting out of your LISP? Write it here:

_____

_____

_____

3. Get into LISP. What is its prompt? Write it here: _____.
Get back out of LISP and log off.

4. Get back into LISP. Enter the integer 3 and a carriage return. Note that LISP types 3 back and issues a prompt. Try 5 this time. Log off.

5. Get back into LISP. Does it have an interrupt key? Write it here: _____. If so get into the break package.

6. What is your break package's prompt? Write it here: _____.

7. How do you get out of the break package? Write it here: _____. Do it! Are you back to the top level?

8. Try going several levels deep in the break package. While in them, try typing a small integer to LISP. Does it echo the integer? Get back to top level again.

9. Does your LISP prefer lowercase or uppercase letters, or doesn't it care? Write the answer here: _____.

10. Log out of LISP and off your system. Take a break.

1.2 Numeric Atoms

The first kinds of S-expressions we will discuss are the two types of *numeric atoms*, fixed-point numbers, and floating-point numbers. They are called *atoms* because, unlike other S-expressions which we will discuss later, they are not decomposable into smaller parts.

Fixed-point numbers are used for normal integers, like 5 or 127. They are typed to LISP just as we normally write integers, except they cannot contain commas or blanks. Thus, we write 54325 rather than 54,325. For a negative integer, just precede the digits by a minus sign, e.g. -5, or -4326. Some LISPs allow you to precede a positive integer with a plus sign. For them, +24 is the same as 24. ALISP, for one, does not allow this.

Fixed-point numbers are different from integers for most LISPs in that there is a largest possible fixed-point number of rather modest magnitude. In ALISP, 123456789 is bigger than the largest fixed-point number. In Franz LISP, however, the biggest integer is extremely large (several thousand or million digits long).

The value of a fixed-point number as an S-expression (every S-expression has a value) is itself. So if we type in a fixed-point number, such as -123, LISP will type it right back at us.

Floating-point numbers are used for numbers with fractional parts and for integers outside the range of fixed-point numbers. A floating-point number looks like a fixed-point number except:

1. It includes a decimal point (.)

and/or

2. It is followed by an exponent of the form Eseee...

where

E signals the exponent part of the number

s is an optional minus sign

eee... is a string of digits

and/or

3. It is outside the range of fixed-point numbers.

The atom sdd.dddEseee represents the decimal number sdd.dddx10^{seee}. For example,

123.45E-2 represents 1.2345

and -.4E12 represents -0.4x10^{12}.

The value of a floating-point number is itself, but LISP always prints floating-point numbers in a standard form with the decimal point just to the left or just to the right of the first significant digit.

Exercises

(From now on, unless otherwise mentioned, all exercises assume you are talking to LISP.)

1. Type some small positive and negative integers, one per line. Note that LISP types them back. Also try zero, and minus zero (a minus sign followed by zero).

2. Try typing +12. Does your LISP treat that as 12, or give an error message? If you typed the period as a decimal point, try again without it.

3. Try the numbers 123.4, -5.6, 0.0000521347, -5678.0000000012345. Type them one per line and see how your LISP responds.

4. Type the *two* numbers 54 325 on *one* line with one or more blanks between them. How does your LISP respond? Some LISPs read only one S-expression per line, others will read more than one.

5. Type 54,325 to LISP. How does it treat a number with a comma in it?

6. Type in the characters 123.4.5E6E-7. If this causes an error

message, write it here:

_____

_____

7. Type a number *preceded* by some blanks. LISP ignores initial blanks on a line.

8. Type the characters 1 2 3 ; 4 5 on a line. The semicolon is the comment character for ALISP and Franz LISP. They ignore it and everything after it on the line. If your LISP has a different comment character, find out what it is and write it here: _____. Try typing 1 2 3 c 4 5, replacing the "c" with your comment character.

9. Does LISP convert the floating-point number 0.0 to the fixed-point 0? Find out by typing 0 . 0 and comparing what LISP types back to how LISP responds when you enter 0. Try - 0 . 0 also.

10. Try typing the numbers 3. and 3 . 0. Are they treated as fixed-point or floating-point numbers?

11. What is your character erase (backspace) character? Some possibilities are BS, #, < -, ^H (remember, that's pressing the H key while holding down the CNTRL key), DEL, RUB. Write yours here: _____. Enter some numbers, using the backspace character to change your mind. Note that it works.

12. What is your line erase character? Some possibilities are BRK, ESC, @ , ^U. Write it here: _____. Enter some numbers, using the line erase character to change your mind. Note how it works.

13. Try entering some very large integers. Does your LISP convert large integers to floating-point numbers? If so, what is your LISP's largest fixed-point number?

14. If *n* is your LISP's largest fixed-point number, is -*n* also a fixed-point number? Can you find an *n* such that -*n* is a fixed-point number, but -($n + 1$) isn't?

1.3 Literal Atoms

LISP was not really designed for numerical work, but for operating on symbols. The most common basic symbol is the *literal atom*. Like numeric atoms, literal atoms are not decomposable. Literal atoms are different from numeric atoms in ways that we will see. When we say "atoms" we will mean both literal and numeric atoms. When we have something to say that holds for only one type of atom, we will be specific.

A literal atom may be a symbol that stands for something that we wish to store information about. For example, the literal atom FRANK may represent some person. Literal atoms are also used as the variables of the LISP programming language.

Although FRANK is a literal atom, we say that the character string F-R-A-N-K is the *print name* or *pname* of the literal atom FRANK, or that the pname of FRANK is "FRANK". We do not speak of a numeric atom as having a pname, only a literal atom. So if we say "the pname of an atom," it should be clear that we are talking about a literal atom.

In Franz LISP, the pname of a literal atom can be any sequence of printable characters except blank, (,), ., [,], ', ¦, ", / as long as the sequence cannot be interpreted as a number. Thus, while 52E3 is a numeric atom in Franz LISP, 52F3 is a literal atom.

In ALISP, the pname of a literal atom must start with an alphabetic character. These are all the printable characters except blank, 0 through 9, the comma, -, ., #, (,), /, ", ', $, @. The rest of the characters in the pname can be alphabetic or numeric. ALISP's numeric characters are 0 through 9, -, ., and #.

Pnames have maximum lengths, but they are very long, typically over 200 characters, so you needn't worry about it.

Since all atoms are S-expressions, literal atoms are too. Unlike numeric atoms, which always evaluate to themselves, literal atoms must be given values by treating them as variables. If you ask LISP to evaluate an atom that does not have a value, it will print an error message. Some atoms have already been given values by the system. The most important atom in LISP is NIL. It has itself as its value. The next most important atom in LISP is T. It also has itself as its value. We will see NIL and T many, many times. You should become good friends with them.

When we want to talk to LISP about a particular atom rather than the atom's value, we can use the quote mark ('). So, for example, if we type in 'FRANK, LISP will type back FRANK. *The value of a quoted S-expression is the S-expression itself.*

Exercises

1. Type in the atoms NIL and T. Note that they evaluate to themselves.

2. Type in the quoted atoms 'FRANK and 'ATOM. Note that a quoted atom evaluates to the atom itself.

3. If you are using ALISP, type in the atom ATOM. What is its value? This is another kind of numeric atom called a *program number* or *PNUM*. There is no way for you to type a PNUM into ALISP, but every atom that is the name of a predefined ALISP function has a PNUM as its value. We will discuss functions later.

4. Type in the atom ∗12Q%. Write the error message you get here:

_____

_____

This error message means that the literal atom you have just asked LISP to evaluate has no value.

5. Type in ′52F3 (or ′52f3 if your LISP prefers lowercase letters). Does your LISP treat that as a literal atom? Compare the results with ′52E3. Now try both without the quote marks. Remember that quoted S-expressions and numeric atoms always evaluate to themselves.

6. Type in the characters ′ABC;DE. Note again the effect of the semi-colon as a comment character. If your LISP uses a different comment character, use it instead of the semicolon here and in the next exercise. (See Exercise 1.2.8.)

7. Now type in ′ABC\;DE. The back-slash means "treat the next char-acter as an alphabetic character." It is called the *escape character*. To get an escape character in a pname, use two in a row, such as ′AB\\CD. Try that. If your LISP has a different escape character (a popular one is "/"), write it here _____, and use it in this exercise, and wherever "\" is used in this text.

8. Type in the atoms 12 and \12. Note that 12 is a number, but that \12 is a literal. The escape character has caused LISP to interpret the 1 as an alphabetic character.

9. In Franz LISP, you can get several strange characters into a pname by surrounding the whole thing with vertical bars. For example, ′|ABC;D(E| is a literal atom, as is ′|53E21|. Try them. Try both |53E2| (without the quote mark) and 53E2.

10. Type in ′AB ′CD on one line. Note again whether your LISP reads one or several S-expressions at a time. Now type in "AB CD. The double quote mark signals the beginning of another kind of atom, the *string*. A string is terminated by another double quote mark. In ALISP, a string is also terminated by a carriage return. A string evaluates to itself. If your LISP has not echoed your string by now, type another double quote. Is the carriage return part of your string? We will not refer to strings much.

11. Enter ′A, then ∗, then ′B, then ∗ again. In ALISP and Franz LISP, the value of ∗ is set to the last value that LISP has printed.

12. Experiment by typing in various quoted atoms whose pnames have all sorts of different characters in them to see how LISP reacts to the different characters.

13. Experiment by typing in various unquoted atoms. Note that most of them don't have values, but some of them do.

1.4 Lists

So far, our collection of S-expressions may be organized as follows:

S-expressions
    Atoms
        Numbers
            Fixed-point
            Floating-point
        Literals
        Strings.

We are now ready to begin discussing non-atomic S-expressions.

The most common kind of S-expression in LISP is the *list*. List processing is, of course, what LISP is all about. As we go along, we will give several different, but equivalent, definitions of the list. The first is: *A left parenthesis followed by zero or more S-expressions followed by a right parenthesis is a list*. Of course lists, as well as atoms, are themselves S-expressions, so **(A (B C) D)** is a list as well as **(A B C D)**. Notice that the parentheses are part of the list; they are not merely grouping brackets as they are in algebra. We refer to the (zero or more) S-expressions in a list as *elements* or *members* of the list. The two lists just shown are different because the first has three elements, the second of which is a list, while the second list has four elements, all of which are atoms. The two lists **(A)** and **((A))** are also different, although the first list is the same as the single element of the second. The most important list is the one with no members—**( )**, called *the empty list* or *the null list*. Some more lists are shown in Table 1.1 with the number of elements they have:

Table 1.1

List	Number of Elements
( )	0
(ATOM)	1
(ALPHA BETA GAMMA)	3
(5 IS A NUMBER "THIS IS A STRING")	5
((A LIST WITHIN A LIST))	1
(( ))	1
((((( )))))	1
(( )( )( )( )( ))	5
(AN (INTERESTING ((LIST) STRUCTURE)))	2

A list is one S-expression regardless of how many S-expressions it contains. So LISP will read one top-level list at a time. That is, after printing a value or upon initial entry to LISP, LISP prints a prompt. You now type a left parenthesis. You are typing in a top-level list until the number of right parentheses you type in equals the number of left parentheses you have typed. Your list may extend over several lines. Some LISPs will type a prompt at the beginning of each line. Others won't. When you finally type a right parenthesis to match that first left parenthesis and then a carriage return, LISP will type the value of the S-expression you entered. Miscounting parentheses can lead to a common, but very frustrating experience. You have typed in too few right parentheses. You think you have entered an entire S-expression and hit the carriage return. LISP, however, just types a prompt (or doesn't even do that) and you both just sit there staring at each other. LISP is waiting for you to finish your S-expression. If you are too confused to finish the S-expression properly and are using ALISP, or any LISP that reads at most one S-expression per line, you should type in a whole lot of right parentheses—more than enough to do the job. If you are using Franz LISP, or most LISPs that read several S-expressions per line, the right bracket,], usually serves as a *super parenthesis* to close all remaining open parentheses.

An easy way to count parentheses is to count "one" at the first left parenthesis, increase the count by one at each subsequent left parenthesis, and decrease the count by one at each subsequent right parenthesis. When you reach "zero" again, you are at the right parenthesis that matches the first left parenthesis and your list is finished. The list below has the appropriate numbers written under each parenthesis.

```
(COUNT () (PARENTHESES (UP) AND)
1        2 1  2           3    2    1

    DOWN (((TILL) YOU REACH) ZERO))
          2 3 4      3            2      1 0
```

Earlier in this section there was a table showing several lists and the number of elements in each one. Count the parentheses of each of these lists until you come out at "zero" for each one.

We will start discussing the values of lists in the next section. For the exercises of this section, you will usually enter a quoted list, which is a list preceded by a single quote mark, such as `'(A ((QUOTED) LIST))`. A quoted list evaluates to the list itself, just as a quoted atom evaluates to the atom itself. If, by mistake, you enter an unquoted list, you will probably get an error message. For practice, count the parentheses of every list you type.

Exercises

1. Type in the quoted list, `'(A ((QUOTED) LIST))`. How does LISP respond? The value of a quoted S-expression is the S-expression itself.

2. Type in the quoted null list: `'()`. How does LISP respond? This is very important! `()` is just another name for the atom `NIL`. `NIL` *is both an atom and the empty list.* Strange, but true.

3. Type in some short unquoted lists and note the error messages. We will discuss them later.

4. Type a line containing just a right parenthesis. How does LISP respond?

5. Type in a quoted list with too many right parentheses. How does LISP respond?

6. Type in `'(EXTRA (LEFT (PARENTHESES]`. Does your LISP use the bracket as a super parenthesis?

7. Type in some quoted lists that extend over several lines. Carefully observe how LISP behaves until the list is finally finished. Note the format in which LISP prints lists.

8. If you are using ALISP, start entering a list, but before finishing, hold down the control key and depress the `S` key (this is the character `CNTRL-S`). Then release the control key and type a carriage return. Note that ALISP prints `*SDEL*` and then a prompt. Now enter `T`. Note that your previous (partial) list has been forgotten. The character sequence `CNTRL-S` followed by a carriage return may be used in ALISP to delete the current list, even if it has gone on for several lines already (try this). If your LISP doesn't have a character for deleting the current list, you may be able to get the same effect by pressing the interrupt character to get into the break package, then getting back to top-level LISP. (See Exercise 1.1.5.) Write your delete-current-list sequence here: _____. You should now be able to delete the last character, delete the current line, or delete the current list.

9. A list can extend over several lines. Can an atom? Type in a quoted list with a carriage return in the middle of one of its atoms. Did LISP interpret that as one atom or as two? Try this with several kinds of atoms. Try typing the escape character right before the carriage return.

10. Where are blanks required and where are they optional? What special characters act as delimiters? Find out by typing in some quoted lists with no blanks between the two outermost parentheses.

11. If your LISP uses brackets as super parentheses, can you also use left

and right brackets like normal parentheses? Do parentheses act like super brackets? Do braces, { }, work?

1.5 Forms and Functions

Since lists are S-expressions, they can be evaluated. Of course, lists are also very useful data structures, so we will often use lists that we never intend to have LISP evaluate. We will distinguish these by referring to lists which we never intend to evaluate as *data lists* and lists which we do intend to evaluate as *forms*. The reason for making this distinction is that a form must satisfy certain restrictions if its evaluation is not to cause an error message. Data lists don't have these restrictions.

Let us now consider functions. We are all familiar with the plus function, which takes two numbers and gives their sum. We are used to writing a particular use of the plus function as two numbers with a plus sign between them, such as $5 + 12$. We can say that $5 + 12$ is an *expression* that *evaluates* to 17. It consists of the plus sign, which names or indicates the plus function, and the two operands or arguments 5 and 12. In LISP, this expression is written as (+ 5 12) or (PLUS 5 12). (Some LISPs use "+", others use "PLUS", and others recognize either. I will use "PLUS" in this book.) Note that (PLUS 5 12) is a form. It is a list whose first element is the name of a function and whose remaining elements are the arguments to that function. The form (PLUS 5 12) can be evaluated by LISP, and evaluates to 17.

Let us now state what we know about the evaluation of lists:

1. If a list is to be evaluated, it must be a form.
2. The first element of a form must name a function.
3. The remaining elements of a form are the arguments of the function.
4. The value of a form is the value of the function applied to the arguments.

So (PLUS 5 12) is a form that evaluates to 17. If you type (PLUS 5 12) to LISP, LISP will type back 17. Remember, however, that if you type '(PLUS 5 12) to LISP, LISP will type back (PLUS 5 12), since '(PLUS 5 12) is a quoted list, and a quoted S-expression always evaluates to the S-expression itself.

What if we want to add several numbers, say 5, 12, 20, and -3? We can give LISP's PLUS an arbitrary number of arguments and it will sum them all up. For example, (PLUS 5 12 20 -3) will evaluate to 34. Some LISP functions take a fixed number of arguments, and some take an arbitrary number of arguments. Using the terminology of ALISP and IN-TERLISP, we will call those that take a fixed number of arguments *SUBR*s and those that take an arbitrary number of arguments *SUBR**s. SUBRs are also sometimes referred to as *spread* functions and SUBR*s as *nospread* functions. SUBRs and SUBR*s are just two of several types of LISP functions. We will discuss some others later.

In order to describe a LISP function we must say several things about it:

1. The name of the function.
2. The type of the function, e.g., SUBR or SUBR*.
3. The number and type of its arguments, e.g., numbers, literals, lists, or general S-expressions.
4. The value that the function returns when applied to its arguments.

We will always do this in a particular format. For example:

(PLUS n_1 ... n_k**)** SUBR*
n_1, ... , n_k must be numbers.
Returns $n_1 + ... + n_k$.

We will not always give all the details in this document, so you should always cross-check with your manual, remembering, however, that manuals always discuss details the novice is not expected to understand. The final determiner of what a function does in your version of LISP is LISP itself. A necessary part of the process of learning a new function is trying it out with a wide variety of arguments.

Exercises

1. Check LISP's responses to **(+ 5 12)**, **(PLUS 5 12)**, **(plus 5 12)**, **+(5 12)**, **PLUS(5 12)**, and **plus(5 12)**. Circle or highlight on the page here those that work, so you can refer back to this page later. If it matters whether you type "PLUS" or "plus", check your answer to Exercise 1.1.9. If typing the function inside the parentheses works, and typing it outside doesn't, you are using an "EVAL LISP," which has become standard, and which I assume in this book. If typing the function outside the parentheses works, and typing it inside doesn't, you are using an "EVALQUOTE LISP," which is not as common as it once was. If both work, I recommend using the EVAL format, unless the experienced LISPers at your installation strongly recommend otherwise. In this book, I will use the EVAL format with uppercase letters. If you use something else, I ask that you "sight transpose," as does the player of a B♭ musical instrument when playing from sheet music written for a C instrument.

2. Compare LISP's responses to **'(PLUS 5 12)** and **(PLUS 5 12)**.

3. Check LISP's response to **(PLUS 5 12 20 -3)**.

4. What is the smallest number of arguments that PLUS will take without giving an error message?

5. What happens if one of the arguments of PLUS is not a number?

6. What happens if some of the arguments of PLUS are fixed-point numbers and some are floating-point?

7. What happens if all the arguments of PLUS are fixed-point numbers, but their sum is too large to be fixed-point? (See Exercise 1.2.13.)

8. Have LISP calculate the following sums:
   a. 2 - 4 + 6 + 8
   b. 1 + 15 - 7 + 23 - 10 - 22
   c. 9 + 11 - 103
   d. 12378659 + 473629867
   e. 3.5 + 7.2 - 23.75 + 53.219

1.6 Forms within Forms

We have seen that the form (PLUS 5 1 2) evaluates to 1 7, and have explained this by saying that the function named by the first element of the list is applied to the remaining elements of the list, which are taken as arguments of the function. But are the arguments the elements of the list or the *values* of the elements of the list? So far it's hard to tell since a number evaluates to itself. Here's a test: will (PLUS 5 (PLUS 8 4)) give an error message since the second argument is a list rather than a number, or will it evaluate to 1 7 since that is the value of 5 added to the value of (PLUS 8 4)? The latter is the case. *SUBRs and SUBR*s always have their arguments evaluated.* Later, we will see other kinds of functions that don't have their arguments evaluated. To avoid confusion, we will say that in the form (PLUS 5 (PLUS 8 4)), "5" and "(PLUS 8 4)" are *argument forms*, while 5 and 1 2 are the *arguments* being passed to PLUS. With a function that doesn't get its arguments evaluated, its arguments are the same as its argument forms. Here is an updated statement on the evaluation of lists:

1. If a list is to be evaluated, it must be a form.
2. The first element of a form must name a function.
3. The remaining elements of a form are the argument forms of the function.
4. If the function is a SUBR or SUBR*, the value of the form is the function applied to the values of the argument forms, which are evaluated in left to right order.

We have been using arithmetic as a familiar domain in which to learn about LISP's evaluation of forms. Let us finish this introduction with a more complete list of arithmetic functions. All of them take numeric atoms as arguments. This is Franz LISP's list. Other LISPs may use different names for some of them. Check your manual.

(ADD1 n) SUBR
  Returns $n + 1$.
(SUB1 n) SUBR
  Returns $n - 1$.
(MINUS n) SUBR
  Returns $-n$.
(FIX n) SUBR
  Converts n to a fixed-point number, truncating if necessary.
(FLOAT n) SUBR
  Returns a floating-point number equal to n.
(DIFF n_1 n_2) SUBR
  Returns $n_1 - n_2$.
(TIMES n_1 . . . n_k) SUBR*
  Returns $n_1 * \ldots * n_k$.
(QUOTIENT n_1 n_2) SUBR
  Returns a floating-point number equal to n_1 / n_2.
(SQRT n) SUBR
  n must be a non-negative floating-point number.
  Returns the square root of n.

For example, the Franz LISP version of $(-7 + \sqrt{(7^2 - 4*2*5)}) / (2*2)$ is

```
(QUOTIENT
   (PLUS 7.0
      (SQRT
         (DIFF (TIMES 7.0 7.0)
               (TIMES 4.0 2.0 5.0))))
   (TIMES 2.0 2.0)).
```

Exercises

1. Evaluate (PLUS 5 (PLUS 8 4)). Does it give an error message or 17?

2. Ask LISP to evaluate (NOTAFUNCTION 5 3). What is the error message when you try to evaluate a list whose first element is not a function? Write it here:

_____

_____

_____

3. Ask LISP to evaluate (PLUS 5 '(PLUS 8 4)). What is the error message when you give a function an argument whose type is wrong? Write it here:

_____

_____

_____

4. Ask LISP to evaluate (SQRT 4 9). What is the error message when you give a function too many arguments? Write it here:

_____

_____

_____

5. Ask LISP to evaluate (SQRT). What is the error message when you give a function too few arguments? Write it here:

_____

_____

_____

6. Try evaluating (DIFF 10 7 3). Is it an error when DIFF is given more than two arguments? If not, is the answer (10-7)-3 = 0; or 10-(7-3) = 6? Try this with QUOTIENT also.

7. Try out your LISP's version of all the functions introduced in this section. Try using fixed-point and floating-point numbers. See if you can get any underflow or overflow error messages.

8. Check if the LISP value of

```
(QUOTIENT
   (PLUS -7.0
         (SQRT
           (DIFF (TIMES 7.0 7.0)
                 (TIMES 4.0 2.0 5.0))))
   (TIMES 2.0 2.0))
```

is the same as your value of $(-7 + \sqrt{(7^2-4*2*5)}) / (2*2)$.

9. Using LISP, find the values of
   a. $(25+30)*15/2$

b. 3.1416*6

c. the average of 5, 6.7, -23.2, 75, and 100.3

1.7 Basic List Processing

Our collection of S-expressions now looks like:

S-expressions
  Atoms
    Numbers
      Fixed-point
      Floating-point
    Literals
    Strings
  Lists
    Data lists
    Forms.

We have discussed how forms are evaluated. We will now start discussing the creation and manipulation of data lists, referred to as *list processing*— what LISP was named for.

The three basic functions for list processing are CAR, CDR, and CONS. Since list processing is what LISP is all about, these are the three most important functions in LISP. "CONS" comes from "CONStruct," and "CAR" and "CDR" from "Contents of the Address part of Register _____" and "Contents of the Decrement part of Register _____," terminology of the IBM 704, on which LISP was first implemented. You needn't remember that. "CAR", "CDR", and "CONS" will become meaningful words to you in their own right.

(CAR list) SUBR
    list must be a non-null list.
    Returns the first element of list.
(CDR list) SUBR
    list must be a non-null list.
    Returns list without its first element.
(CONS s list) SUBR
    list must be a list. s can be any S-expression.
    Returns list with s added as the first element.

A more schematic way of explaining these three functions is:

$$(CAR \ '(s_1 \ . \ . \ . \ s_k)) = s_1$$
$$(CDR \ '(s_1 \ s_2 \ . \ . \ . \ s_k)) = (s_2 \ . \ . \ . \ s_k)$$
$$(CONS \ 's_1 \ '(s_2 \ . \ . \ . \ s_k)) = (s_1 \ s_2 \ . \ . \ . \ s_k).$$

This leads us to *the LISP identities*:

```
(CAR (CONS s list)) = s
(CDR (CONS s list)) = list
(CONS (CAR list) (CDR list)) = list
     (if list is not NIL)
```

and to a second way of defining what a list is (compare the definition in Section 1.4):

1. NIL is a list.
2. If L is a list and S is an S-expression, then (CONS S L) is a list whose CAR is S and whose CDR is L.
3. Nothing else is a list.

Here are some more examples:

```
(CAR '(1 2 3)) = 1
(CDR '(1 2 3)) = (2 3)
(CONS 1 '(2 3)) = (1 2 3)
(CAR (CDR '(1 2 3))) = 2
(CONS (CAR (CDR '(1 2 3)))
      (CDR (CDR '(1 2 3)))) = (2 3)
(CAR '(((((()))))) = (((NIL)))
(CAR (CAR '((A B) C))) = A
(CDR (CAR '((A B) C))) = (B)
(CONS '() '(A B C)) = (NIL A B C)
(CONS '(A B C) '()) = ((A B C))
(CDR '(A)) = NIL
(CONS NIL NIL) = (NIL).
```

Forms of the form (CxR (CyR (CzR L))) where x, y, and z are each either "A" or "D" are so common that we can abbreviate them (CxyzR L). So, for example, we have the following:

first element of the list L = (CAR L)
second element of the list L = (CADR L)
third element of the list L = (CADDR L).

Some LISPs allow any number of "A"s and "D"s to be used in this way; others allow only three, four, or some other small number.

Exercises

1. How does your LISP respond to (CAR NIL)? To (CDR NIL)? Remember that NIL and () *are the same thing.*

2. How does LISP respond to giving CONS an atom instead of a list as its second argument, e.g., (CONS 'A 'B)? This is another S-

expression called a *dotted pair*, which is not used much. For the time being, if you ever see a dotted pair it will be because you have made a mistake.

3. Compare your LISP's response to (CONS 'A (CONS 'B 'C)) with its response to (CONS 'A (CONS 'B NIL)). The former, sometimes called a *dotted list*, is not a true list because its CDDR is an atom other than NIL. Again, for the time being, if you ever see a dotted list it will be because you have made a mistake.

4. Check all the examples given in this section. Count parentheses.

5. There are 14 functions whose names are formed by a "C", an "R", and 1 to 3 "A"s and "D"s in between, namely:

1. CAR	3. CAAR	7. CAAAR	11. CADDR
2. CDR	4. CADR	8. CAADR	12. CDADR
	5. CDAR	9. CADAR	13. CDDAR
	6. CDDR	10. CDAAR	14. CDDDR

Try out all these functions on the list '(((A B) (C D) E) (F G) (H) I) and on other examples until you can predict the value of each of them applied to any list structure.

6. How many "A"s and "D"s does your LISP allow between "C" and "R"? Write the number here: _____.

1.8 The Function QUOTE

We have been using the quote mark, as in 'A or '(1 2 3), since Section 1.3. Actually, the quote mark is an abbreviation of a use of the LISP function QUOTE, which is a different kind of function from those we have discussed so far. QUOTE is an FSUBR. Like SUBRs, FSUBRs take a fixed number of arguments, but their arguments are given to them unevaluated! They control the evaluation of their own arguments. QUOTE is rather simple. It returns its unevaluated argument as is—unevaluated.

(QUOTE s) FSUBR
    Returns the unevaluated S-expression s unevaluated.

Note that the effect is just what you're used to. For any S-expression s, the value of (QUOTE s) is s itself. (QUOTE A) is exactly equivalent to 'A. '(1 2 3) is exactly equivalent to (QUOTE (1 2 3)).

Exercises

1. Type in 'A and (QUOTE A); also '(1 2 3) and (QUOTE (1 2 3)). Note the equivalence.

2. Type in (QUOTE '(1 2 3)) and '(QUOTE (1 2 3)). What does your LISP type back?

3. Type in '(1 2 '(A B) 3) and (QUOTE (1 2 (QUOTE (A B)) 3)).

4. Type in ''A and (QUOTE (QUOTE A)). Did you predict what happened?

Chapter 2

Programming in Pure LISP

2.1 Defining Your Own Functions

Although there are quite a few functions provided by the LISP system, you will want to define your own. Indeed, a LISP program is nothing but a collection of functions written by the LISP programmer.

To define a function, you use a special function-defining function. Different LISPs give this function different names, but they all act essentially the same. Some versions are summarized below:

UCI LISP and ALISP	`(DE fn varlist form)`
Franz LISP, MACLISP, and Zetalisp	`(DEFUN fn varlist form)`
INTERLISP	`(DEFINEQ` `((fn varlist form)))`

In all these cases, `fn`, `varlist`, and `form` are not evaluated; `fn` must be a literal atom, `varlist` must be a list of literal atoms, and form must be a `form`. I will use `DE` in this text since it requires the least amount of typing.

`DE` returns `fn`, but its main use is that it has the side-effect of defining `fn` to be the name of a function whose formal arguments are the atoms in `varlist` and whose definition is `form`. Let's consider an example:

```
(DE LIST3 (S1 S2 S3)
    (CONS S1 (CONS S2 (CONS S3 NIL))))
```

has the effect of defining the function `LIST3`, which takes three S-expressions as arguments and returns a list whose members are those S-expres-

21

sions. After evaluating this DE, the S-expression (LIST3 'A '(B C) 'D) would evaluate to (A (B C) D). The choice of the atoms S1, S2, and S3 for the formal arguments of LIST3 (In LISP terminology, we say that S1, S2, and S3 are *lambda variables* of LIST3. We will see why in the next section.) is completely arbitrary. We could have chosen almost any three literal atoms, but there are some bad choices. NIL and T are never good choices for lambda variables, and in some LISPs, ALISP in particular, any atom that is the name of a function is a bad choice for a lambda variable.

Functions defined by DE are called EXPR or LAMBDA functions. This type of function is characterized by

1. being programmer defined
2. taking a fixed number of arguments
3. having its argument forms evaluated.

When an EXPR is called, e.g., when LISP is asked to evaluate the form (LIST3 'A '(B C) 'D), the following happens:

1. LISP checks that CAR of the form names a function, and finds that it is an EXPR.
2. The argument forms are evaluated left to right.
3. The values of the argument forms become the values of the corresponding lambda variables. (We say that the variables are *bound to* the values of the arguments.)
4. The form in the definition of the EXPR is evaluated.
5. The lambda variables are unbound—returned to their previous states.
6. The value of the form in the definition becomes the value of the original form.

Let us follow our example through the process:

1. LIST3 is found to be an EXPR.
2. 'A evaluates to A, '(B C) to (B C), and 'D to D.
3. S1 is bound to A, S2 to (B C), and S3 to D.
4. (CONS S1 (CONS S2 (CONS S3 NIL))) is evaluated. Note that the atoms S1, S2, and S3 have values during this evaluation. The value of this form is (A (B C) D).
5. S1, S2, and S3 return to their previous values (possibly none).
6. (A (B C) D) is returned as the value of (LIST3 'A '(B C) 'D).

This is the first time that we have seen an atom get a new value. *The primary method by which an atom gets a value is to be bound as a lambda variable*. We should not use T or NIL as lambda variables because we always want them to have themselves as values.

We can define the function FIRST to be synonymous with CAR:

↗(DE FIRST (L) (CAR L))

and a function SECOND to be synonymous with CADR:

↗(DE SECOND (L) (FIRST (REST L))).

Here we used the function REST, which is not defined. *We can use an undefined function in the definition of a function, as long as we define it before asking LISP to evaluate a form which has it as the* CAR. We can now define REST to be synonymous with CDR.

(DE REST (L) (CDR L))

Notice that it is an error to give SECOND an atom or a list with fewer than two elements. Our documentation of SECOND should indicate this:

(SECOND list) EXPR
     list must be a list of at least two elements.
     Returns the second element of list.

Exercises

1. What is the format of the function-defining function for your LISP? Write it here:

   _____

2. Define the function LIST3 as given in this section, and test it on several different groups of arguments.

3. Check the values of S1, S2, and S3 both before and after a call to LIST3. Notice that, even though they have values within LIST3, they have no values either before or after.

4. Evaluate (LIST3 'A B 'C) and (LIST3 A B C). Notice that the error messages show you in what order the arguments are evaluated.

5. Define and test the function FIRST as given in this section.

6. Define SECOND as given in this section and try it out *before* defining REST. The error occurs when LISP tries to evaluate the form (REST L). Of course, this happens after L has been bound to the actual argument. If your LISP has put you in its break package, check this by typing in L. Then get out of the break package, and ask for the value of L again. The break package allowed you to interact with LISP

inside the environment of the function call. This is a very valuable debugging aid.

7. Now define REST, test REST, and test SECOND again.

8. You can observe LISP evaluating a set of functions by using the trace package. In many LISPs, this consists of the two FSUBR*s TRACE and UNTRACE. (TRACE fn_1 . . . fn_k) turns on the tracing of functions fn_1, . . . , fn_k. (UNTRACE fn_1 . . . fn_k) turns them off. Evaluate (TRACE FIRST SECOND REST), then (SECOND '(A B C)). Note that when each function is called, its arguments are printed, and when it returns, its value is printed. Also note that each trace print is labeled so you can tell which value goes with which call. Now evaluate (UNTRACE FIRST SECOND REST) and (SECOND '(A B C)) again. The tracing has been turned off.

9. Define the functions THIRD through TENTH, each returning the obvious element of a long enough list. (Hint: The definition of TENTH need be no longer than the definition of SECOND.) Use the tracing facility to watch some of these in action.

10. Define the function (SQR n), which returns the square of the numeric atom n.

11. Using FIRST, SECOND, and CONS, define the function (SWAP L) to return the two-element list L with its two elements interchanged. Make sure that (SWAP '(A B)) returns the list (B A), rather than the dotted pair (B . A). After making sure that your SWAP works with two-element lists, see what happens if you give it longer and shorter lists, or atoms.

12. Using FIRST, SECOND, THIRD, and LIST3, define the function (REVERSE3 L) to return the reverse of the three-element list, L. For example, (REVERSE3 '(A B C)) should evaluate to (C B A).

2.2 Looking at Function Definitions—LAMBDA

We have seen how to define a function, but after defining one and trying it out, we may want to look at its definition again. This may simply be because we want to study it or show it to a friend, or it may be because we want to define another function like it, or one that uses it, or one that it uses and we haven't written yet. Most often we need to look at the definition because our tests have shown that it is not quite correct, and we need to study it to decide what is wrong so that we can correct it.

Chances are, the definition we typed on the terminal is no longer visible, so we need to ask LISP to retrieve the definition for us and show it to us. Certainly LISP has stored the definition somewhere where it can be found when we use the function. Different LISPs store function definitions in different places, and have different functions for retrieving them.

Two kinds of function definition retrieval functions are common. The first kind consists of functions that simply retrieve and return the function definition. Since the function definition is returned, it is printed on the terminal as part of the regular top-level LISP cycle. A function definition is a list, so the definition returned is printed like any other list. A long definition may extend over several lines, just like a long list may, and may be difficult to read. The other kind of function definition retrieval function prints the definition in a nicely indented format that is easy to read. The value of this kind of function is just as irrelevant as the value of the function-defining function. It is just used for the effect of printing the definition. We will call functions of the first kind "definition access" functions and of the second kind "pretty-printing" functions.

A common definition access function is the SUBR GET. If we wanted to see the definition of the function LIST3, which we defined in the last section, and GET was our definition access function, we would enter (GET 'LIST3 'EXPR), and LISP would return the definition. You may read this form as "GET the definition of LIST3 as an EXPR." We must include EXPR in the form because GET is actually a more general function than simply a function definition access function, but this is the only use we have for it for now. UCI LISP and MACLISP are two of the dialects that use GET as the definition access function. Another common definition access function, used by Franz LISP and INTERLISP, is a specialized GET called GETD. In LISPs that use GETD, we would retrieve the definition of LIST3 by entering (GETD 'LIST3). You may read this as "GET the Definition of LIST3." Sometimes, the specialized GET has a different name. For example, in Zetalisp, we would enter (FSYMEVAL 'LIST3).

Some LISPs, in particular ALISP, store function definitions as the value of the function name. In these LISPs, we would get the definition of LIST3 simply by typing LIST3 to top-level LISP.

For long function definitions, it is better to use the pretty-printing function, if your LISP has one. Even for short definitions, it is sometimes quicker to type a call to the pretty-printing function than to the definition access function. Typically, the pretty-printing function is an FSUBR, so it is not necessary to type a quote mark before the function name. In Franz LISP, UCI LISP, and INTERLISP the pretty-printing function is PP, so in these LISPs we could see the definition of LIST3 by entering (PP LIST3). In ALISP, we would enter (PPRINT LIST3), and in Zetalisp we would enter (GRINDEF LIST3).

In any case, if we ask to see the definition of LIST3, we will see

(LAMBDA (S1 S2 S3) (CONS S1 (CONS S2 (CONS S3
NIL)))).

The atom LAMBDA that is the CAR of this list comes from Church's
lambda calculus, a formal presentation of the theory of functions. In LISP,
it signifies that the list of which it is the CAR is an EXPR. The CADR of
the lambda expression is a list of the formal arguments of the EXPR. It
is because the definition of every LISP EXPR is a lambda expression that
we refer to the formal arguments as "lambda variables."

In some LISPs, a lambda expression is also a form that evaluates to
itself. So in these LISPs, the value of (LAMBDA (L) (CAR (CDDDR
L))) is (LAMBDA (L) (CAR (CDDDR L))). However, in all
LISPs, an unquoted lambda expression may be the CAR of a form. For
example, ((LAMBDA (L) (CAR (CDDDR L))) '(A B C D
E)) is a valid form and evaluates to D. We can now give a more complete
rule about the evaluation of lists (compare with the beginning of Section
1.6):

1. If a list is to be evaluated, it must be a form.
2. The CAR of a form must be the name of a function, or a lambda
    expression, or (in some LISPs) evaluate to a function definition.
    If not, an error message is given.
3. The CDR of the form is a list of the arguments of the function.
4. If the function is an SUBR, an SUBR* or an EXPR, the arguments
    are evaluated, in most LISPs, in left to right order.
5. The value of the form is the result of applying the function indi-
    cated by its CAR to the elements (evaluated, if called for) of its
    CDR.

Not only should you now have a better understanding of the evaluation of
forms, but you should now know how to ask LISP to show you the definition
of a function you have previously defined, and you should feel comfortable
reading that definition.

Exercises

1. Define LIST3 (not necessary if you have not left LISP since doing
    Exercise 2.1.2). Find out what your definition access function is, and
    write it here:

    _____

    Have LISP show you the definition of LIST3.

2. Does your LISP have a pretty-printing function? If so, write its name
    here:

    _____

    Have LISP pretty-print your definition of LIST3. It may be too short
    to extend over several lines.

3. Look at the definitions of some other function you have defined.

4. What happens if you ask LISP for the definition of some predefined functions such as CAR and COND? (If GET is your definition access function, try (GET 'CAR 'SUBR) and (GET 'COND 'FSUBR).) Try both your definition access function and your pretty-printing function.

5. What is the value of the form (LAMBDA (L) (CAR (CDDDR L)))?

6. What is the value of the form
(CLAMBDA (L) (CAR (CDDDR L)))
'(A B C D E))?

7. What error message do you get when trying to evaluate a form whose CAR is neither a function name nor a lambda expression? Write it here:

_____

_____

_____

8. The CAR of a form can be the name of a function or a lambda expression. Can it be a form that evaluates to the name of a function? To find out, try ((CADR '(CADR CDR CAR)) '(A B C)).

9. Can the CAR of a form be a form that evaluates to a lambda expression? To find out, try ((LIST3 'LAMBDA '(L) '(CADR L)) '(A B C)).

10. Can the CAR of a form be an atom that does not name a function, but which is bound to a function name, a lambda expression, or a form which evaluates to one of those? To find out the answer for your LISP, define the functional APPLY1. A functional is a function that takes a function as an argument.

```
(APPLY1 F A) EXPR
      Returns the value of applying the function F to the S-expression
      A.
(DE APPLY1 (F A) (F A))
```

Try evaluating

```
(APPLY1 CAR '(A B C))
(APPLY1 'CAR '(A B C))
(APPLY1 ADD1 (PLUS 5 7 9))
(APPLY1 'ADD1 (PLUS 5 7 9))
```

```
(APPLY1 (LAMBDA (L) (CAR (CDDDR L)))
        '(A B C D E))
(APPLY1 '(LAMBDA (L) (CAR (CDDDR L)))
        '(A B C D E))
(APPLY1 (LIST3 'LAMBDA '(L) '(CADR L))
        '(A B C D))

(APPLY1 (CADR (LIST3 CADR CDR CAR))
        (LIST3 'A 'B 'C))

(APPLY1 (CADR '(CADR CDR CAR))
        (LIST3 'A 'B 'C))
```

11. Trace APPLY1, and try again those forms that worked in the previous question. (If any did.) Carefully note what F was bound to in each case. Formulate a more complete and accurate rule for the evaluation of forms for your LISP than was given in this section.

12. Define and test the function (QUAD-ROOTS a b c) that takes three numbers a, b, and c and returns a list of the two roots of the quadratic equation, $ax + bx + c = 0$. That is:

$$\left(\frac{-b + \sqrt{(b^2 - 4ac)}}{2a} \quad \frac{-b - \sqrt{(b^2 - 4ac)}}{2a} \right)$$

Use your function SQR. Also define and use as a "help" function (DISCRIM a b c) which returns $\sqrt{(b^2 - 4ac)}$. See Exercise 1.6.7 for an example. Make sure your function returns a list rather than a dotted pair. Use tracing and pretty-printing as tools to help you debug your functions if they don't work correctly the first time.

2.3 Saving for Another Day

If you define some functions and want to save them for a future session, either because you feel they are useful or because you have to interrupt your session, you can do so by putting them on a *file*. There are two basic methods used by LISPs for doing this. With the first method, you put LISP DE forms on a text file with any text editor provided with your computer system. The editor is the same one you would use to type letters, papers, or programs in any other programming language, and the file is like any other file with one of these documents on it. The only difference is that this file contains a series of LISP forms looking just like they would if you typed them into top-level LISP. Then, when you are in LISP, there is a function which will read and evaluate the forms in such a file just as if you were typing them yourself. The result of this is that the functions defined by the forms in the file are now defined and available for use. The text file itself can be saved on a disk, and used again and again, perhaps weeks and months after you first typed it. If your LISP works this way, you will have to learn how to use the editor and the file system on your own; they are beyond what I can discuss in this text. We will refer to this method as the *text file method*.

The second method of saving function definitions on files is to have specially formatted LISP files which can be created, written to, and read from from within LISP. With this method, you define functions as you have already been doing. When you want to save some of them on a file, you use some special LISP functions to create a file, and to put the definitions you want on the file. These files are saved on a disk even after you leave LISP and terminate your computing session. At some subsequent session, when you are back in LISP, and want to use the functions you saved, there is another special function which will load the definitions from the file and make them available again. Typically, these files should not be edited with a regular text editor because the special format might be disturbed. We will, therefore, refer to them as *LISP files*, and to this method of saving functions as the *LISP file method*.

These are the two basic methods for saving function definitions for future sessions, but each dialect of LISP has its own idiosyncrasies. I will discuss some of them in some detail to give you a feel for the possibilities. You will have to consult your own manual to learn how your LISP works.

Franz LISP uses the text file method, although packages of functions which allow the LISP file method are commonly included. If you have a file named MYFILE in which you have typed a sequence of DEFUN forms (remember, Franz LISP uses DEFUN instead of DE), you can make the functions defined there available by typing (LOAD 'MYFILE) to top-level LISP. Actually, the common convention is to give such files names ending in ".L", so you would probably name your file MYFILE.L instead. Since Franz LISP knows about this convention, when you enter (LOAD 'MYFILE), it will first look for a file named MYFILE.L, and only if it doesn't find it will it look for a file named simply MYFILE. If you use this convention, you can also load your file by entering (LOAD 'MYFILE.L). Remember, MYFILE.L must be prepared, and changed if necessary, with a standard text editor. We will discuss editors some more in Section 2.6. You should also know how to look at MYFILE.L on your terminal, and how to get a hard copy of it on some printer. These are also topics you should be familiar with from more general uses of your particular computer system.

ALISP uses the LISP file method. You create an ALISP file by evaluating (INITFILE filename), where filename is any LISP atom which satisfies the system's rules for file names. Since INITFILE is an FSUBR, you don't need to use QUOTE.

You can then put function definitions on your file by evaluating (OUTPUT filename (function₁ . . . functionₖ)). Again, no QUOTE is needed, but notice that the second argument of the FSUBR, OUTPUT, is a *list* of function names. The definitions of the functions listed will then be written onto the file. If any function is already on the file, the file version will be replaced by the current definition. If you redefine a function that is on a file and you want to keep the file current, you must OUTPUT it again.

When you want to retrieve your function definitions, just evaluate (INPUT filename) and all the functions stored on that file will be defined just as if you retyped them. If you only want to retrieve selected functions from the file, evaluate (INPUT filename (function₁ . . . functionₖ)) and only the listed functions will be retrieved. Notice that INPUT is an FSUBR* which can take either one or two arguments.

To see the function definitions stored on the file, type (GRIND filename) and they will be typed out on your terminal. GRIND is an FSUBR* that takes one to four arguments. The first must be the name of the ALISP file to be listed. The other three are keywords that can appear, if used, in any order. They are:

ALPHA: The functions are listed in alphabetical order.
XREF: A cross reference is listed, showing, for each func-
              tion in the file, all other functions in the file which
              use it.
DISPOSE: The file is listed on the line printer rather than on
              your terminal.

For example, if we have an ALISP file named MYFILE, evaluating (GRIND MYFILE ALPHA XREF DISPOSE) will send to the line printer a pretty-printed listing of all functions in MYFILE, in alphabetical order, followed by a cross reference table.

We have put the ALISP file package into our version of Franz LISP. Similarly, your local installation may have added to your dialect's file packages.

INTERLISP also allows the LISP file method. To establish MYFILE as a file of function definitions, do (MAKEFILE 'MYFILE). Then, to tell INTERLISP that you want the definition of the function FOO to be put on MYFILE, do (ADDTOFILE 'FOO 'MYFILE 'FNS). At a later session, you can have all the functions on MYFILE available again by doing (LOADEFS T 'MYFILE), or selected functions input by doing (LOADEFS '(function₁ . . . functionₖ)

'MYF I LE). If, after loading the file, you redefine any of the functions on it, INTERLISP will automatically take care of making sure that the latest version of each of those functions is on MYF I LE.

Exercises

1. Does your LISP use the text file or the LISP file method of saving functions in files?

2. If your LISP uses the text file method, how would you load the functions stored in MYF I LE? Write the form here:

   _____

3. If your LISP uses the LISP file method, how would you create the file MYF I LE? Write the form here:

   _____

4. If your LISP uses the LISP file method, how would you put the definition of the function F OO in MYF I LE? Write the form here:

   _____

5. If your LISP uses the LISP file method, how would you load the definitions stored in MYF I LE? Write the form here:

   _____

6. If your LISP uses the text file method, create a file named MYF I LE, and type in definitions for L I ST3, APPLY1, QUAD-ROOTS and DISCRIM.

7. If your LISP uses the LISP file method, enter LISP, create a file named MYF I LE, define L I ST3, APPLY1, QUAD-ROOTS, and DISCRIM, and put these definitions in MYF I LE.

8. List MYF I LE on your terminal. You might be able to do this from within LISP, or you might have to use the standard file listing command of your operating system. Make sure your four functions are there.

9. If you are now in LISP, get out of it. In fact, log off the system. Then log back on, and get into LISP. Load your functions from MYF I LE. Make sure their definitions are correct.

10. Change the definition of one of your functions. Now leave LISP, get back in, and load the file again. Which definition is now in force? Make sure you can change a function definition permanently in your file.

11. If your LISP can load a selected list of functions from a file, do so, but misspell one of your function names. How does LISP tell you that one of the functions you requested was not loaded?

12. How can you add comments to your file? If your LISP uses the text

file method, you can do so by typing in lines beginning with the comment character (see Exercise 1.2.8) or by putting the comment character followed by your comment at the end of a line. If your LISP uses the LISP file method, you may have a special function for adding a comment to a particular function on a particular file, or you may have a special QUOTE-like function which you can "call" in your function definitions between the list of lambda variables and the form. An example of this latter technique might be:

```
(DE LIST3 (S1 S2 S3)
    (COMMENT RETURNS A LIST OF THE THREE
             S-EXPRESSIONS S1 S2 AND S3)
    (CONS S1 (CONS S2 (CONS S3 NIL))))
```

Write your LISP's technique for commenting files here:

_____

_____

13. Add comments to your file, MYFILE.

14. Cause your file to be printed on a line printer. Now log off and go find your listing.

2.4 Predicate Functions

So far, the functions we have used, whether provided by LISP or defined by us, have returned numbers, lists, or parts of lists. There are also functions that return "true" or "false," useful, for example, for asking "Is the S-expression an atom?" or "Is this an empty list?" In some programming languages, these functions are called "logical functions" or "Boolean functions." We call them *predicate functions*.

One of the most basic LISP predicate functions is ATOM, a SUBR of one argument which can be any S-expression. If s is an atom, the value of (ATOM s) is the atom T, signifying "true." Remember that T is one of the two literal atoms that evaluate to themselves. If s is not an atom (i.e., it's a list), the value of (ATOM s) is NIL, signifying false. That's right, NIL *is an atom and the empty list and LISP's way of saying "false."*

Some other basic predicate functions are:

> (NUMBERP s) SUBR
> > Returns T if the S-expression s is a numeric atom,
> > NIL otherwise.

(FIXP s) SUBR
> Returns T if s is a fixed-point number,
> NIL otherwise.

(FLOATP s) SUBR
> Returns T if s is a floating-point number,
> NIL otherwise.

(ZEROP n) SUBR
> Returns T if n is the number zero,
> NIL otherwise.

(GREATERP n1 n2) SUBR
> n1 and n2 must be a numeric atoms.
> Returns T if n1 is greater than n2, NIL otherwise.

(EQ s1 s2) SUBR
> Returns T if s1 and s2 are identical S-expressions.

EQ returns T if its two arguments are the same literal atoms. So the value of (EQ 'A 'A) is T, as is the value of (EQ 'B (CADR '(A B C))). (In some LISPs, EQ also returns T if its two arguments are numerically equal fixed-point numbers. In others, a special equality predicate, such as = or EQP is used.) However, even though the two arguments of (EQ '(A) '(A)) look the same, they are not *identical*. They are two different lists that just happen to have the same elements, and so the value of (EQ '(A) '(A)) is NIL. EQ should never be used to compare lists, only atoms.

Modern LISPs have many functions predefined, but there are relatively few functions that *need* to be predefined. The rest may be defined using those few. Modern LISPs evolved by people defining useful functions and saving them in files. These people's friends also found the functions useful. Eventually, the functions were compiled and made a part of the standard local LISP. Then that LISP was sent to friends at other locations, and it eventually congealed into a dialect. Different dialects differ because they have had slightly different histories. Nevertheless, good ideas tend to arise independently, or to spread by word of mouth and be implemented slightly differently. This is why all LISPS have a core of identical functions, and a periphery of different and slightly different functions.

Since most LISP functions can be (and once were) defined in LISP, an excellent way to explain a LISP function is to show its LISP definition. I will be doing this more and more as we proceed. If your LISP already has one of these functions defined as an SUBR, you may use it without redefining it. If not, you may define it as an EXPR. Therefore, if I show the definition of a function that I think is likely to be defined already, I will document it as a "____R" instead of an "SUBR" or an "EXPR." (As we progress, you may also see ____R*s, F____Rs, and F____R*s.)

Some LISPs don't mind if you redefine predefined functions. Others may get quite messed up by this. Nevertheless, it is often educational to try out our own definitions of predefined functions. The safe way is to use the name MYfn instead of fn. For example, we could define MYCADR by (DE MYCADR (L) (CAR (CDR L))), or MYZEROP by (DE MYZEROP (N) (EQ N 0)).

With all this said, let's look at some often-predefined functions:

> (NULL S) ____R
> > Returns T if S is NIL, NIL otherwise.
> > (DE NULL (S) (EQ S NIL))

NULL is used to see if a list is empty. Since NIL is also the logical value "false," the logical function NOT is easy to define.

> (NOT S) ____R
> > Returns T if S is NIL, NIL otherwise.
> > (DE NOT (S) (NULL S))

> (MINUSP N) ____R
> > Returns T if the numeric atom N is less than zero
> > NIL otherwise.
> > (DE MINUSP (N) (GREATERP 0 N))

> (PLUSP N) ____R
> > Returns T if the numeric atom N is greater than zero,
> > NIL otherwise.
> > (DE PLUSP (N) (GREATERP N 0))

> (LISTP S) ____R
> > Returns T if S is a non-empty list, NIL otherwise.
> > (DE LISTP (S) (NOT (ATOM S)))

Since we have the function GREATERP, can we define the function (LESSP N1 N2) to be true if N1 is less than N2? N1 is less than N2 if N1 is neither GREATERP than N2 nor EQ to N2. To write this definition, we need predicate functions like "and" and "or." LISP has these functions. They are both FSUBR*s.

Like SUBRs, SUBR*s, and FSUBRs, FSUBR*s are precompiled LISP functions. Like SUBR*s, FSUBR*s take an arbitrary number of arguments. Like FSUBRs, FSUBR*s get these arguments unevaluated and they control the order of evaluation of the arguments. Table 2.1 summarizes the comparison of these four types of precompiled functions.

Table 2.1

	Gets arguments evaluated	Gets arguments unevaluated
Fixed number of arguments	SUBR	FSUBR
Arbitrary number of arguments	SUBR*	FSUBR*

LISP's AND and OR functions work in this way:

> (AND s₁ . . . sₙ) FSUBR*
>   Returns NIL if the value of any sᵢ is NIL.
>   Otherwise, returns the value of sₙ.

> (OR s₁ . . . sₙ) FSUBR*
>   Returns NIL if the values of all sᵢ are NIL.
>   Otherwise, returns the value of the first sᵢ whose
>   value is not NIL.

Notice that instead of returning either NIL or T, AND and OR return either NIL or some non-NULL S-expression. As we will see in the next section, LISP treats any value other than NIL as a true value, not just T.

AND and OR have the interesting feature that they evaluate their arguments only until they can figure out the answer. That is, as soon as one argument of AND evaluates to NIL, NIL is returned without evaluating the rest of the arguments. Similarly, as soon as one argument of OR evaluates to a non-NULL value, that value is returned without evaluating the rest of the arguments. This is particularly useful if an error would result from blindly evaluating all the arguments. For example, (AND (NUMBERP X) (GREATERP X 5)) evaluates to T if X is a number greater than 5 and to NIL if X is either not a number or is a number not greater than 5. In particular, (AND (NUMBERP 'A) (GREATERP 'A 5)) evaluates to NIL even though (GREATERP 'A 5) would produce an error if evaluated.

Since we have AND, OR, and NOT, we can define more complicated predicates. For example, LESSP:

> (LESSP N1 N2) EXPR
>   Returns T if N1 is less than N2, NIL otherwise.
>   (DE LESSP (N1 N2)
>   (NOT (OR (EQ N1 N2)
>   (GREATERP N1 N2))))

Exercises

1. Evaluate `(ATOM 'A)`, `(ATOM '(A))`, `(ATOM 12)`, `(ATOM 'CAR)`, `(ATOM CAR)`, `(ATOM (CAR '(A B)))`, and `(ATOM (CDR '(A B)))`.

2. Try out `NUMBERP`, `FIXP`, `FLOATP`, `ZEROP`, and `GREATERP`. Be sure to try each with a variety of arguments. In particular, try `(ZEROP 0)`, `(ZEROP 0.0)`, `(ZEROP -0)`, AND `(ZEROP -0.0)`. If your LISP is missing some of these functions, see if it has something similar.

3. Evaluate `(EQ 'A 'A)` and `(EQ 'B (CADR '(A B C)))`.

4. Evaluate `(EQ 25 (PLUS 20 5))`. If your LISP doesn't use `EQ` for fixed-point numbers, find out what it does use and write it here: _____. Check that it considers 25 equal to `(PLUS 20 5)`.

5. Evaluate `(EQ '(A) '(A))`.

6. Define `MYCADR` and `MYZEROP`, and test them.

7. Test `NULL` and `NOT`. (They should already be defined.) Can you detect any difference between them?

8. Test `MINUSP` and `PLUSP`. Do they work as expected? Be sure to test them on zero as well as on other numbers, including floating-point numbers.

9. Does your LISP have `LISTP` predefined? If so, does it agree with the one in this section? Is `'()` a list? Is `'NIL` an atom? Remember, `'()`, `()`, `'NIL`, and `NIL` are all the same! Try them with `EQ`. Try `ATOM` and `LISTP` with each. Chances are your `ATOM` will return T. In that case, the `LISTP` of this section will return `NIL`. Define `MYLISTP1` as `LISTP` is defined here, and define `MYLISTP2` so that it will return T for any list, even the empty one. Which way does your LISP's `LISTP` work? Does it have both versions?

10. Test `(AND NIL NIL NIL)`, `(AND NIL T NIL)`, `(AND FOO NIL)`, `(AND NIL FOO)`, `(AND T FOO)`, `(AND FOO T)`, and `(AND 1 2 3)`.

11. Test `(GREATERP 'A 5)`. It should give an error message. Try `(AND (NUMBERP 'A) (GREATERP 'A 5))` and `(AND (GREATERP 'A 5) (NUMBERP 'A))`.

12. Define `(NUMBER-GREATER-THAN-5 S)` to return T if S is a number greater than 5, and `NIL` if S is not a number, or is a number not greater than 5. Test it on small and large numbers, and on non-numeric S-expressions.

13. Test (OR T T T), (OR T NIL T), (OR FOO T), (OR T FOO), (OR NIL FOO), (OR FOO NIL), and (OR 1 2 3).

14. Define and test MYLESSP as LESSP is defined in this section. Does it agree with your LISP's LESSP?

15. Define and test a function that returns True if its one argument is a single-digit integer, NIL otherwise. (By "True" I mean any non-NULL value.)

16. Define and test a function that returns True if its one argument is a list of exactly one element, NIL otherwise.

17. Define and test a function, VARIABLEP, that returns True if its one argument is the atom whose print name is a question mark, NIL otherwise. That is, (VARIABLEP '?) evaluates to True.

18. Define and test the function (MATCH-ATOM A1 A2) so that it returns True if either A1 or A2 is a variable (as defined by VARIABLEP), or if they are EQ.

19. Change VARIABLEP so that it recognizes any numeric atom to be a variable. Without changing MATCH-ATOM, it should now be the case that (MATCH-ATOM 'A 1) is True and (MATCH-ATOM 'A '?) is NIL. Save VARIABLEP and MATCH-ATOM in a file called MATCHING for use in later exercises.

2.5 COND

One of the two most powerful features of any programming language is the *conditional*—a way of saying, "if this then that else this other." LISP's conditional is the FSUBR* COND. The format of a COND form is: (COND (p₁ e₁) . . . (pₙ eₙ)). That is, COND takes an arbitrary number of arguments, each of which is a list of two elements, referred to as COND *pairs*. COND first evaluates p_1. If p_1 evaluates to NIL, COND moves on to the next COND pair. COND evaluates the CAR of each COND pair until one (the kth, say) evaluates to anything other than NIL (i.e., to True). COND then evaluates e_k, the second element of that pair, and returns its value as the value of the COND form. If all p_1 evaluate to NIL, the value of the COND form will be NIL and no e_1 will be evaluated. Notice that:

1. At most one e_i will be evaluated.
2. No p_i will be evaluated after the first that evaluates to True.
3. The value of the COND form is always the value of the last sub-expression that is evaluated.

4.   When COND evaluates the p_i, NIL is treated as false, and
anything else is treated as True.

The last point is a general rule in LISP, which we first mentioned in the
last section. *LISP treats NIL as the logical value false and anything else as
the logical value True.* The atom T is only one of LISP's True values,
returned by predicate functions when there is nothing more useful to return.

In most programming languages, if-then-else is a kind of statement. In
LISP, COND is an expression, but it is like if-then-else. Notice the simi-
larity:

```
if b₁, then s₁                    (COND (p₁ e₁)
else if b₂ then s₂                      (p₂ e₂)
else if b₃ then s₃                      (p₃ e₃)
else s₄                                 (T e₄))
```

Since T always evaluates to T, which is not NIL, if p_1, p_2, and p_3 evaluate
to NIL, the value of the COND will be the value of e_4, just as s_4 will be
executed if b_1, b_2 and b_3 are false.

Let's look at some simple functions which we can define using COND:

```
(ABSVAL N) EXPR
      Returns the absolute value of the number N.
      (DE ABSVAL (N)
         (COND ((MINUSP N)(MINUS N))
               (T N)))
```

ABSVAL is already available in some LISPs.

```
(HAS-EXACTLY-ONE-ELT L) EXPR
      Returns T if the list L has exactly one element,
      NIL otherwise.
      (DE HAS-EXACTLY-ONE-ELT (L)
         (COND ((NULL L) NIL)
               (T (NULL (CDR L)))))
```

Notice that this function returns NIL if L is either empty or has a non-
empty CDR. Also notice that (CDR L) is evaluated only if (NULL L)
has returned NIL. *Never take the CAR or the CDR of a list unless you
have already ascertained that the list is not empty.* Notice also that if HAS-
EXACTLY-ONE-ELT is given an atom other than NIL, it will cause
an error. This is all right since the comment says that L must be a list. If
it had said that L could be any S-expression, the function should not cause
an error, regardless of the type of its argument.

Exercises

1. Define MYABSVAL as given in this section. Try it out with positive and negative fixed-point and floating-point numbers and with zero.

2. Enter the definition of HAS-EXACTLY-ONE-ELT. Try it out with NIL, a list of one element, a list of several elements, a non-NIL atom. Compare it with your solution to Exercise 2.4.13.

3. Define HAS-EXACTLY-TWO-ELTS. Pretty-print its definition. Try it out with an appropriate set of test cases.

4. Define LITP. (LITP S) should return True if S is a literal atom and NIL if S is any other S-expression.

5. Define the function DONT-CARE to do what VARIABLEP did in Exercise 2.4.14, that is, return True if its argument is '?. Load VARIABLEP and MATCH-ATOM from the file, MATCHING, created in Exercise 2.4.16. Redefine (MATCH-ATOM A1 A2) to return True if the two arguments are EQ or either argument is '?; if either argument is a variable (as recognized by VARIABLEP), MATCH-ATOM should return a list whose CAR is the variable and whose CADR is the other argument; otherwise, MATCH-ATOM should return NIL. Save DONT-CARE and the revised MATCH-ATOM in MATCHING along with VARIABLEP.

2.6 Editing LISP Functions

As your LISP functions become longer, it becomes bothersome to retype them in their entirety to correct an error. It is easier to take the current version of the function and change only those parts that need changing. This can be done with an *editor*. Just as there are two different ways that LISPs handle files, the text file method and the LISP file method (see Section 2.3), so there are two approaches to editing functions.

LISPs that use the text file method tend to assume that your function definitions are in some file. If you have to change one, you use the standard, system-supplied text editor to do so. You must get out of LISP, into the editor, edit the function you want to change, get back into LISP, and reload the functions in the file, including the one you changed. Actually, modern LISPs and the operating systems they run on make this easier. You can generally move from LISP to the editor directly, without losing what you have been doing, and then get back into LISP where you left off. As mentioned in Section 2.3, there are sometimes functions for reading just a specific function from a text file, so you don't have to reread all the functions you have not changed.

If your LISP uses the text file method, you should already be familiar with the editor and how to use it from Section 2.3.

LISPs that use the LISP file method generally have built-in editors that are specifically LISP oriented, in that instead of dealing with lines and characters, they deal with lists and atoms. Usually there is an FSUBR, perhaps ED I T, which you call with the name of the function you want to edit. Having done this, you are no longer talking to LISP, but are talking to the LISP editor, and the specific subject under discussion is the lambda expression which forms the definition of the function. The language you use to talk to the editor is not necessarily the same as the language you use to talk to LISP (that of S-expressions), but may be a special-purpose command language which you use to get the editor to do things with the S-expression already understood to be under discussion.

Editor command languages can be as extensive and sophisticated as full-fledged programming languages, so the way to learn them is the same. Start by learning a small set of commands—just enough to get by with. Soon you will be able to use them when necessary without looking them up each time. Every few months, review the editor manual to see if there is a command you haven't used before but whose usefulness you can immediately see. Add this command to your repertoire. The idea is not to become an expert in the full editor immediately, but to get a set of tools that enable you to do your work easily.

If you are using a LISP file to store your function definitions, remember that when you leave the editor, chances are that the definition on the file is still the old one. Some LISPs will automatically update the file after you edit a function stored there, some will do this updating when you leave a LISP session for all functions you edited during the session, but others won't do any automatic updating, and you must remember to do it yourself.

Some LISPS that use the text file method also have built-in LISP editors for use with functions not stored in files, and for quick editing during debugging. If your LISP is like this, you may want to try out both editing methods to see which you find more comfortable. Also see what more experienced LISPers around you do.

Below is a list of an adequate beginning set of LISP editor commands showing the specific commands for our version of Franz LISP. If your LISP has a LISP editor, look in your manual, and on each line below put your LISP's command for each function, if it has one.

1. Begin editing the function FN: (EDITF FN)

    _____

2. Print the S-expression under discussion: PP, P, and ?

    _____

3. Change the subject to the second element of the current list: 2

    _____

4. Add the S-expression S before the fourth element: $(- 4 \quad S)$

5. Add the S-expression S after the last element: $(N \quad S)$

6. Delete the third element: (3)

7. Replace the fifth element with S: $(5 \quad S)$

8. Replace all instances of the S-expression A with B within the current S-expression: $(R \quad A \quad B)$

9. Remove the pair of parentheses around the second element: $(B0 \quad 2)$

10. Enclose the second through the fourth elements in a list by adding a matching pair of parentheses: $(BI \quad 2 \quad 4)$

11. Change the discussion to the list enclosing the current one: 0

12. Change the discussion to the topmost list: ^

13. Terminate the editor and return to LISP: OK

Remember, you learn by practicing, and even if you make a mistake nothing disastrous will happen.

Exercises

1. The remaining exercises of this section assume you are using a LISP editor. If you are using a text editor, make sure you can do the following: put a function definition on a file; get into LISP and load the function from the file; get back into the editor and change the function definition; get back into LISP and load the new definition.

2. Define the function FN as $(DE \quad FN \quad (L1 \quad L2) \quad (CONS \quad (CAR \quad L1) \quad (CDR \quad L2)))$. Enter the editor to edit FN. Print the definition. Leave the editor.

3. Again begin editing FN. Print the current S-expression. Do the following. After each step, print the current S-expression.

    A. Change all occurrences of L1 to A1.
    B. Change the discussion to the list of lambda variables, $(A1 \quad L2)$.

C. Add L3 as the third lambda variable.
D. Change the discussion back up one level.
E. Change the discussion to the list (CONS (CAR A1)
    (CDR L2)).
F. Remove the parentheses around the second element, chang-
    ing the list to (CONS CAR A1 (CDR L2)).
G. Now change it to (CONS CAR A1 REVERSE (CDR
    L2)).
H. Add parentheses, so it becomes (CONS CAR A1
    (REVERSE (CDR L2))).
I. Change the second element, so it becomes (CONS CONS
    A1 (REVERSE (CDR L2))).
J. Add parentheses, so it becomes (CONS (CONS A1
    (REVERSE (CDR L2)))).
K. Add a new element, so it becomes (CONS (CONS A1
    (REVERSE (CDR L2))) (CDDR L3)).
L. Change the discussion back up to the full definition of FN.
M. Terminate the editor and take a look at your new FN.

2.7 Recursion

At the beginning of Section 2.5, we said, "one of the two most powerful
features of any programming language is the *conditional*." The other is
some method for repeating a computation over and over until some condition is found. This gives us a lot of computation for a relatively small
amount of text. One such method is called *recursion*.

The definition of a LISP function contains a form. The CAR of the form
is also a function. Some arguments of the form may be embedded forms,
which also involve functions. We say that these functions are *used by* the
function being defined, or that the function being defined *uses* these functions. For example, the function ABSVAL, defined in Section 2.5, uses
MINUSP and MINUS. A function that uses itself is called a *recursive
function*. The use of recursive functions is called *recursion*.

Does it make sense to use a function in its own definition? Sure! Remember what was said in Section 2.1: "*We can use an undefined function
in the definition of a function, as long as we define it before asking LISP
to evaluate a form which has it as the* CAR". When we define a function
using itself, it is undefined just until we finish the definition. By the time
we ask LISP to evaluate a form with it as the CAR, it is already defined.
So everything is O.K.

To continue the discussion, let's have an example. Using only ZEROP,

ADD1, and SUB1, let's define the function SUM that returns the sum of two non-negative integers. (Some LISPs use SUM as the name of their addition function.)

```
(SUM N1 N2) ____R
     Returns the sum of the two non-negative
     fixed-point numbers, N1 and N2.
(DE SUM (N1 N2)
   (COND ((ZEROP N1) N2)
         (T (SUM (SUB1 N1) (ADD1 N2)))))
```

Evaluating (SUM 3 5) causes the evaluation of (SUM 2 6), which causes the evaluation of (SUM 1 7), which causes the evaluation of (SUM 0 8), which finally returns 8. What if we evaluated (SUM 10000 100)? The rather short definition of SUM would cause a lot of computation.

Each call of SUM causes another, recursive, call of SUM, until finally SUM is called with a first argument of 0. (From now on, we will say "calling" a function, rather than "evaluating a form whose CAR is" a function.) This causes a value to be returned, and the computation terminates. When defining a recursive function, we must make sure that, for every intended set of arguments, the computation will eventually terminate. A recursive function whose evaluation never terminates is called *infinitely recursive*. The process is called *infinite recursion*. If you ask LISP to evaluate a form that causes infinite recursion, LISP will not return to you until it encounters a time or space limit. Your entire LISP session might even be terminated by the operating system. Needless to say, defining an infinitely recursive function is a mistake.

It is easy to avoid defining an infinitely recursive function if you observe the standard pattern of recursive function definitions:

1. Every recursive function is of the form (DE fn varlist (COND cond-pairs)).
2. The first COND pair always tests for a terminal condition and gives a result that does not require a recursive call of the function being defined.
3. The last COND pair uses the function being defined.
4. The COND pairs should be in increasing order of the amount of work they might require. (I call this the law of laziness.) Specifically, all COND pairs that use the function being defined come after all those that don't.

5. Each recursive use of the function being defined must somehow bring the computation closer to the termination condition.

Our definition of SUM obviously satisfies points 1-4. To see that it also satisfies point 5, note that the termination condition is that the first argument is zero, that each time SUM is called the first argument is decremented by one, and that since the first argument is both a fixed-point number (an integer) and positive, repeatedly subtracting one from it will eventually cause it to be zero. Before calling a recursive function, you should assure yourself that it will terminate. Usually this is fairly easy. Also, it is usually fairly easy to convince yourself that the definition is correct. This involves checking termination, checking that every case is considered, and checking that every case is correct. In our SUM example, we already checked termination. A non-negative integer is either zero or positive and these are the two COND pairs, so every case is considered. The first case is correct because for any n_2, $0 + n_2 = n_2$. The second case is correct because for any positive n_1 and any n_2, $n_1 + n_2 = (n_1 - 1) + (n_2 + 1)$. Since all cases are handled correctly, our definition of SUM must be correct!

Exercises

1. Define MYSUM as we have in this section. Pretty-print it and read it carefully to make sure it looks correct. Try it out with several examples. Question: Which examples should you use? Answer: At least one example for each COND pair, and the examples should be tried in the same order as the COND pairs appear.

2. Trace your function MYSUM and follow it closely while evaluating (MYSUM 3 5). Turn off the trace.

3. Try MYSUM with some large integers as its first argument. Can you find an integer so large that an error occurs? Write the error message here:

_____

This is the same error you will get if a function you write is infinitely recursive. The error occurs when a large number of recursive calls are made, but before an infinite number have been made (of course).

4. LISP has probably put you into the break package. Evaluate the atoms N1 and N2. Their values are what they are bound to in the most recent call of MYSUM.

5. Get out of the break package, and back to top-level LISP. (See Exercise 1.1.7.) Notice that the computation is aborted.

6. Sometimes a computation we ask LISP to do takes so long that we suspect infinite recursion without being certain. The thing to do in that case is to interrupt LISP, get into the break package, and examine where LISP is and what is happening. In many LISPs, we interrupt a computation by pressing the same interrupt key used to get into the break package when LISP is waiting at the top level for input (see Section 1.1), but in some LISPs a different interrupt key is used. Once LISP is interrupted, it enters the same break package you saw in Section 1.1 and in Exercise 4 above. There are now two different ways to leave the break package: jumping back to top level without completing the computation, as you did in Exercise 5 above; or continuing the computation from where it was interrupted. Look in your manual, or ask your instructor or a more experienced friend for the following:

a. the key to interrupt a computation

---

b. the way to continue a computation after an interruption

---

c. the way to cancel the computation after an interruption

(In Franz LISP, the three answers are: ^C; (RETURN T); and ^D.)

7. Try MYSUM with a first argument large enough that there is a noticeable time before the value is printed, but not so large that an error is caused. Now do this again, but before LISP prints the value, press the interrupt key. Evaluate the atoms N1 and N2 to see how far the computation has reached. Leave the break package by continuing the computation. Check that the answer is correct, and has not been affected by the interruption.

8. Try the same MYSUM example, and again press the break key before it finishes. Look at N1 and N2 again. Are you in the same place you were before? (The chances of that are slim.) Now get back to top level without finishing the computation.

9. Ask LISP to evaluate (MYSUM -4 3). You are now in an infinite recursion. (What element of our argument that SUM terminates has broken down?) Press the interrupt key to see how far LISP has gotten. Return to LISP's top level without finishing the computation (especially since you never would).

10. Define a different version of SUM as follows:

```
(DE SUM2 (N1 N2)
  (COND ((ZEROP N1) N2)
        (T (ADD1 (SUM2 (SUB1 N1) N2))))).
```

Does SUM2 always give the same answer as MYSUM for the same arguments? Trace (SUM2 3 5). Note carefully the difference between the ways MYSUM and SUM2 compute the answer. MYSUM accumulates its answer in one of its arguments "on the way down" and does no computation "on the way up." SUM2 seems to peel apart the problem on the way down, collecting a "stack" of computations, and then constructs the answer on the way up. This latter approach is actually more common than the former among recursive functions.

11. Using only ZEROP, SUB1, and either MYSUM or SUM2, define the recursive function MYPRODUCT that multiplies two non-negative integers. Carefully make sure that your function works correctly. Trace MYPRODUCT and your SUM function to see how they work together.

12. Using only ZEROP, SUB1, and MYPRODUCT, define the function (POWER N I) to return the value of N raised to the I th power assuming that N and I are non-negative integers. Remember, defining a new function includes designing it, convincing yourself that it will work, typing it into LISP, asking LISP to pretty-print it out, carefully reading it for typing errors, possibly editing it, trying it with an adequate set of examples, and repeating the last four steps until it's correct.

13. Try POWER with reasonably large arguments, and interrupt LISP before the answer is printed. Another useful thing to see in the break package is a list of all the functions that have been called and not yet finished. In Franz LISP and MACLISP, you can see this list by evaluating (BAKTRACE). In INTERLISP, you just enter the atom BT. How do you do it in your LISP? Write it here:

_____. Try it. In what order are the functions listed? In most LISPs it will be the most recently called function first. The ability to interrupt a computation and look around in whatever environment you find yourself is a very useful debugging tool. While in the break package, you may ask LISP to evaluate any S-expression, and you may look at the stack of functions that have been called. Your LISP manual may describe other things you can do in your break package, but some of them may be too sophisticated for you right now.

2.8 Recursion on Lists, Part 1—Analysis

In the last section, we wrote recursive functions that operated on integers. We saw that recursive functions must be written so that every recursive call brings one of the arguments closer to the termination condition. With integers, the termination condition is usually ZEROP, and either SUB1 (for positive integers) or ADD1 (for negative integers) will always bring an integer closer to zero.

In this section, we will start writing recursive functions that operate on lists. The termination condition for lists is always NULL, and CDR will always bring a list closer to NIL. For our first function, let's write LENGTH, which will count how many elements a list has. We use the same pattern we used in the last section:

1. Termination condition: The LENGTH of NIL is 0
2. Recursive case: The LENGTH of a non-NULL list is one more than the LENGTH of its CDR.

So our definition is:

```
(LENGTH L) ____R
        Returns the number of elements in the list L.
        (DE LENGTH (L)
          (COND ((NULL L) 0)
                (T (ADD1 (LENGTH (CDR L))))))
```

Notice that this will always terminate and that every case (there are only two) is correct, so the definition must be correct.

There were only two COND pairs in LENGTH because LENGTH always recurses all the way to the NULL termination condition. Often there is a second termination condition which can allow the recursive function to stop before NIL is reached. This usually involves some property of the CAR of the list. A good example of this is:

```
(MEMBER A L) ____R
        Returns T if A is an element of the list L,
        NIL otherwise.
        (DE MEMBER (A L)
          (COND ((NULL L) NIL)
                ((EQ A (CAR L)) T)
                (T (MEMBER A (CDR L)))))
```

Notice the pattern again. The test for NIL is first, because NULL is always the final termination condition for lists and because we must check that L is not NIL before looking at its CAR. The only COND pair involving recursion is last. The definition must be correct because it always terminates, and every case is correct: A is not an element of NIL; A is an element of any list whose CAR is EQ to A; if the CAR of a non-NULL list is not EQ to A, A is an element of the list just in case it is an element of the CDR of the list. Since a list only has a CAR and a CDR, there is no other place for A to hide. (Remember, we do not consider X to be an element of the list '((A) B (C X D) E).)

MEMBER stopped as soon as it could return T, and returned NIL only when it had searched the whole list. Some functions reverse this pattern. Consider:

(LATP L) EXPR
        Returns T if all members of the list L are atoms,
        NIL otherwise.

```
        (DE LATP (L)
          (COND ((NULL L) _____)
                ((LISTP (CAR L)) NIL)
                (T (LATP (CDR L)))))
```

Again, the test for NIL is first. As soon as we find one member that is not an atom, we can return NIL without looking any further. If (CAR L) is an atom, we can return T only if (LATP (CDR L)) is T. But what should we return if L is NIL? Is NIL a list of all atoms? Asked just like that, the answer is not obvious, but consider (LATP '(A)). Since 'A is an atom, the value of (LATP '(A)) is the value of (LATP NIL). But the value of (LATP '(A)) *should be* T. Therefore, the value of (LATP NIL) *must be* T. This is a not uncommon situation: we want to define a function on lists, but it's not obvious what its value should be for NIL, so we write it to handle the other cases properly and look at the definition to see what its value should be for NIL. Our resulting definition is

```
        (DE LATP (L)
          (COND ((NULL L) T)
                ((LISTP (CAR L)) NIL)
                (T (LATP (CDR L))))).
```

This definition reads strangely, since it doesn't use ATOM. We could replace (LISTP (CAR L)) by (NOT (ATOM (CAR L))). That would be less strange, but still cumbersome. At the cost of bending our rules a bit, we could write

```
(DE LATP (L)
   (COND ((NULL L) T)
         ((ATOM (CAR L)) (LATP (CDR L)))
         (T NIL))).
```

That reads so much better that we will stick with it. Readability concerns often lead us to interchange the last two COND pairs, but readability is important since we want our functions to reflect how we think about our problems. Consider the situation if we had wanted to write a function that "returns NIL if any member of the list L is itself a list, T otherwise." Which definition would be better for this?

Now let us write a function to test if two lists have the same length. An easy way is:

```
(EQ-LENGTH1 L1 L2) EXPR
    Returns T if the lists L1 and L2 have the same length,
    NIL otherwise.
    (DE EQ-LENGTH1 (L1 L2)
       (EQ (LENGTH L1) (LENGTH L2)))
```

The trouble with this definition is that both lists must be examined in their entirety. If one list has five elements and the other has 10,000, this seems like a lot of extra work. Let's try a different version that stops as soon as the shorter list is exhausted. This is the method of comparing two piles of stones if you don't know how to count. Keep throwing away a pair of stones—one from each pile—until either pile is empty. If the other pile is now empty, both piles had the same number of stones in them. Otherwise, they didn't.

```
(EQ-LENGTH2 L1 L2) EXPR
    Returns T if the lists L1 and L2 have the same length, NIL
    otherwise.
(DE EQ-LENGTH2 (L1 L2)
   (COND ((NULL L1) (NULL L2))
         ((NULL L2) NIL)
         (T
          (EQ-LENGTH2 (CDR L1) (CDR L2)))))
```

The only difference between EQ-LENGTH2 and the pattern we've seen earlier is that here we are recursing on two arguments simultaneously.

Even though the second element of the first COND pair is not a constant, it is a form whose evaluation does not involve recursion.

Exercises

1. Enter the definition of MYLENGTH. Test it with every example from the beginning of Section 1.4. Trace some small examples.

2. Evaluate (MYLENGTH 'A). Note that the error message means you have incorrectly passed a list processing function a non-list.

3. Enter the definition of MYMEMBER. Test it and trace some examples. Try out (MYMEMBER 'X '((A) B (C X D) E)).

4. Enter the definition of LATP and test it.

5. Enter the definitions of EQ-LENGTH1 and EQ-LENGTH2. Test them out and compare traces.

6. Some LISPs have a timing function, perhaps called TIME or RUNTIME, that will evaluate a form, and print out how many milliseconds it takes to run. If your LISP has such a function, write its name here: _____. Compare the running times of EQ-LENGTH1 and EQ-LENGTH2 when one argument has five elements and the other has ten, and again when one has five elements and the other has 100.

7. In some LISPs, the value of (MEMBER 11 '(2 3 5 7 11 13 17)) would be (11 13 17) rather than T. Redefine (MYMEMBER A L) so it returns either the first tail of L whose CAR is EQ to A, or NIL in case L does not contain A.

8. Does your LISP have MEMBER predefined? If so, which version?

9. Define the function (COUNT A L) to return the number of times that the atom A appears as an element of the list L. (Hint: Two of three COND pairs will cause recursion.)

10. Define the function (EQ-LAT L1 L2), where L1 and L2 are lists of atoms (all elements are atoms) and EQ-LAT returns T if the corresponding elements of L1 and L2 are EQ but NIL if they are not. (Hint: In my version, only the third of four COND pairs causes recursion.)

11. Define the function (NTH N L), where N is an integer and L is a list, to return the N-th member of L.

12. Define the function (NEGNUMS L) to return T if L is a list all of whose members are negative numbers, NIL otherwise.

13. In your MATCHING file (see Exercise 2.5.5), define the function (MATCHLAT L1 L2) to be like EQLAT except it considers the

atom ′? (recognized by DONT-CARE) to be "EQ" anything. For example, (MATCHLAT ′(A ? C D E) ′(A B C ? E)) should return T.

14. Define (PAIRED-WITH A LPAIRS), where A is an atom, LPAIRS is a list of pairs of atoms, and PAIRED-WITH returns the first atom, B, that is paired with A in LPAIRS. For example, (PAIRED-WITH ′Y ′((X FIRST) (Y SECOND) (Z THIRD))) should return SECOND. If A is not the CAR of a pair in LPAIRS, PAIRED-WITH should return NIL. Add PAIRED-WITH to your MATCHING file.

15. Define the function (RAC L) to return the last element of the list L.

16. Define the function (LAST-NUMBER L), which returns the last element of the list L that is a number. For example, (LAST-NUMBER ′(1 A 2 3 B 4.5 C D)) returns 4.5. If no element of L is numeric, LAST-NUMBER should return NIL. (Hint: Use the help function (LAST-NUMBER1 L PREVIOUS), which returns the atom PREVIOUS if no element of L is a number, the last number in L otherwise.)

17. Define the function (RIGHT-MOST L ATOMS), which returns the right-most element of the list L that is in the list of atoms ATOMS, or NIL if no element of ATOMS is in L. For example, (RIGHT-MOST ′(5 + 2 - 3) ′(- +)) returns the atom -. (You may need an escape character before the "-" to make LISP treat "-" as an alphabetical character. See Exercise 1.3.7.) Save this function on a file named COMPUTE for use in later exercises.

2.9 Recursion on Lists, Part 2—Synthesis

In Exercise 2.7.10, we saw that there were two kinds of recursive functions. One kind might perform some computations "on the way down," but once it finds an answer, it just returns it, doing no computation "on the way up." The other kind collects a "stack" of computations on the way down, and constructs its answer on the way up. If you look carefully at the functions we dealt with in Sections 2.7 and 2.8, you will see that the only ones that did any construction on the way up returned numbers. We will now consider recursive functions that construct lists.

Remember that the basic list construction function is CONS, which builds a list from an S-expression and a list. CONS will be at the heart of recursive list construction functions. Remember also that the basic list—on top of which all others are built—is NIL, the empty list.

The simplest recursive list construction function is:

```
(COPY L) ____R
        Returns a copy of the list L.
(DE COPY (L)
   (COND ((NULL L) NIL)
         (T
            (CONS (CAR L) (COPY (CDR L)))))).
```

Notice that COPY pulls apart the list on the way down and puts it back together on the way up. Although dull by itself, COPY shows the basic pattern of list synthesis functions. Strangely, COPY is useful enough that it is predefined in many LISPs. We'll look at it some more in the exercises.

Let's next write a function that strings together two lists:

(APPEND '(A B C) '(D E F)) should return (A B C D E F), (APPEND () '(D E F)) should return (D E F).

```
(APPEND L1 L2) ____R
        Returns a list consisting of the members of L1
        followed by the members of L2.
(DE APPEND (L1 L2)
   (COND ((NULL L1) L2)
         (T (CONS (CAR L1)
                  (APPEND (CDR L1) L2)))))
```

Compare this with SUM2 in Exercise 2.7.10. Note the analogies APPEND:SUM2, NULL:ZEROP, CONS(CAR L1):ADD1, CDR:SUB1.

LISP lists have a strange asymmetry about them—the first element is easier to get at than the last. This asymmetry becomes apparent when we try to write a function to reverse a list. (REVERSE '(A B C)) should be (C B A). It is not as easy to write as COPY was, but we can use APPEND:

```
(REVERSE L) ____R
        Returns a copy of L with the order of elements
        reversed.
(DE REVERSE (L)
   (COND ((NULL L) NIL)
         (T (APPEND (REVERSE (CDR L))
                    (CONS (CAR L) NIL)))))
```

The second argument of APPEND must be (CONS (CAR L) NIL) rather than just (CAR L) because both arguments of APPEND must be lists.

A second way of writing REVERSE is interesting because it illustrates a common pattern. It is easy to write a function REVERSE2, which takes two lists, and appends the reverse of its first argument to its second argument:

```
(REVERSE2 L1 L2) EXPR
      Returns a list consisting of the elements of L1 in
      reverse order followed by the elements of L2 in
      original order.
(DE REVERSE2 (L1 L2)
   (COND ((NULL L1) L2)
         (T
            (REVERSE2 (CDR L1)
                      (CONS (CAR L1) L2))))))
```

Notice that REVERSE2 is to SUM (Section 2.7) exactly what APPEND is to SUM2. Given REVERSE2, we can easily write a second version of REVERSE, called REVERSE1:

```
(REVERSE1 L) EXPR
      Returns a copy of L with the order of elements
      reversed.
(DE REVERSE1 (L) (REVERSE2 L NIL))
```

REVERSE1 does nothing on its own. It just initializes REVERSE2's second argument to be NIL. REVERSE2 would actually be a strange function to call with a non-null second argument. It really just serves as a "help function" for REVERSE1. A common situation— the helper does all the work.

Comparing REVERSE with REVERSE1 (we include REVERSE1's helper, of course), we see that REVERSE is very inefficient. Look at the recursive form (APPEND (REVERSE (CDR L)) (CONS L NIL)). The recursive call to REVERSE pulls (CDR L) apart and pastes it together in reverse order only to have APPEND pull it apart and paste it together again. REVERSE1, on the other hand, "visits" each element of its list only once.

So far, we have essentially been copying lists. A simple complication is to make substitutions in a list:

```
(SUB-FIRST NEW OLD L) EXPR
      Returns a copy of L with the atom NEW replacing the first
      occurrence of the atom OLD.
(DE SUB-FIRST (NEW OLD L)
   (COND ((NULL L) NIL)
         ((EQ (CAR L) OLD)
            (CONS NEW (CDR L)))
```

```
(T
 (CONS
  (CAR L)
  (SUB-FIRST NEW OLD (CDR L))))))
```

Finally, a third COND pair has appeared. The pattern is a combination of what we saw in the last section with what we have been seeing in this section. As soon as we find OLD as the CAR of L, we can return a value. If we never find it, we eventually get the null list and return NIL. In either case, we paste back the earlier CARs on the way up.

We can use lists to represent sets. Let a *set* of atoms be a list of atoms in which no two atoms are EQ and for which order is irrelevant. A list in which order is irrelevant but atoms can appear multiple times is called a *bag*. Let's write a function to turn a bag into a set:

```
(MAKESET BAG) EXPR
       Returns a set containing just those elements in
       bag BAG.
(DE MAKESET (BAG)
   (COND ((NULL BAG) NIL)
         ((MEMBER (CAR BAG) (CDR BAG))
          (MAKESET (CDR BAG)))
         (T (CONS (CAR BAG)
                  (MAKESET (CDR BAG))))))
```

Note that both the second and third COND pairs involve recursion, but only the third pair involves explicit list construction. The second pair just recurses down the bag ignoring the CAR. Compare this with your definition of COUNT from Exercise 2.8.9.

The union of two sets S1 and S2 is a set which contains every element that is in S1 or in S2, and only those elements. The definition of UNION is similar to that of MAKESET.

```
(UNION S1 S2) EXPR
       Returns the union of the sets S1 and S2.
(DE UNION (S1 S2)
   (COND ((NULL S1) S2)
         ((MEMBER (CAR S1) S2)
          (UNION (CDR S1) S2))
         (T (CONS (CAR S1)
                  (UNION (CDR S1) S2)))))
```

Exercises

1. Enter the definition of MYCOPY and test it. See if your LISP has COPY, and if so, if it does the same thing as ours.

2. Is a list ever EQ to a COPY of itself? Try it. EQ tests for identity. A list and its COPY are equal in some sense, but not identical. We will pursue this in the next section.

3. Enter and test the function MYAPPEND. See if your LISP has APPEND, and if so, how it is defined.

4. Define (NCARS N L), where N is an integer and L is a list at least N elements long. NCARS should return a list whose elements are the first N elements of L. For example, (NCARS 3 '(A B (C D) E F)) = (A B (C D)). Some LISPs already have a function like NCARS.

5. Define (NCDRS N L), where N is an integer and L is a list at least N elements long. NCDRS should return a list whose elements are the elements of L omitting the first N. For example, (NCDRS 3'(A B (C D) E F)) = (E F).

6. Evaluate:

```
((LAMBDA (L) (EQ (NCARS (LENGTH L) L)
                 (NCARS (LENGTH L) L)))
  '(A B C)).
```

The moral is that NCARS makes a copy of its list.

7. Evaluate

```
((LAMBDA (L) (EQ (NCDRS 0 L) (NCDRS 0 L)))
  '(A B C)).
```

NCDRS does not make a copy of its list. Is this also true if you replaced 0 by some positive integer?

8. Evaluate

```
((LAMBDA (L1 L2)
   (EQ (NCDRS (APPEND L1 L2) (LENGTH L1))
       L2))
  '(A B C) '(D E F)).
```

Note that APPEND does not make a copy of its second argument. What about its first argument?

9. Define and test MYREVERSE and REVERSE1. Compare their running times on some long list. (See Exercise 2.8.6.)

10. Define and test SUB-FIRST.

11. Define SUBST* to be like SUB-FIRST but to replace *all* top-level occurrences of OLD by NEW. For example, (SUBST* 'X 'Y '(A B Y (X Y) Z Y)) = (A B X (X Y) Z X). See if your LISP has a function like SUBST*.

12. Define and test MAKESET.

13. Define and test UNION.

14. The intersection of two sets, S1 and S2, is the set consisting of those elements that are in S1 and also in S2. Define INTERSECTION.

15. The relative complement (set difference) of two sets, S1 and S2, is the set consisting of those elements of S1 which are not also in S2. Define SET-DIFF.

16. A set S1 is a subset of a set S2 if every element of S1 is a member of S2. Define (SUBSET S1 S2) to return T if the set S1 is a subset of the set S2, NIL otherwise.

17. Two sets are equal if they have exactly the same elements. Define (EQUAL-SETS S1 S2) to return T if S1 and S2 are equal sets, NIL otherwise. Make sure the order of elements in a set is irrelevant and that the order of the two arguments of EQUAL-SETS is irrelevant.

18. The cross product of two sets, S1 and S2, is the set S3, which consists of pairs such that the first of each pair is a member of S1 and the second of each pair is a member of S2, and S3 contains all such pairs. Define (XPROD S1 S2) to return the cross product of the sets S1 and S2. For example, (XPROD '(A B) '(C D E)) should evaluate to ((A C) (A D) (A E) (B C) (B D) (B E)) or any other ordering of these six pairs. (Hint: Use a help function XPROD1 that takes an element and a set and returns a list of pairs. For example, (XPROD1 'A '(C D E)) would return ((A C) (A D) (A E)).)

19. Define (LEFT-ARG EXPR OPS) to return a copy of the list EXPR up to, but not including, the right-most occurrence of any atom in the list OPS. For example, (LEFT-ARGS '(5 + 2 - 3) '(- +)) should return (5 + 2). (Hint: Use a help function.) Add this function to your file named COMPUTE.

20. Define (RIGHT-ARG EXPR OPS) to return that part of the list EXPR following the right-most occurrence of any atom in OPS. For example, (RIGHT-ARG '(5 + 2 - 3 * 2) '(- +)) should return (3 * 2). Also add this function to COMPUTE.

21. Add to your MATCHING file a function (MATCH PAT LST),
where PAT and LST are both lists of atoms. MATCH should return
a list of all pairs (V A) where V is a variable (recognized by
VARIABLEP) in PAT and A is the corresponding atom in LST. If
the *n*th element of PAT is not a variable, it must be EQ to the *n*th
element LST. Otherwise, MATCH should return NIL. If no element
of PAT is a variable, but each is EQ to its corresponding element of
LST, MATCH should return ((T T)). If a variable occurs more
than once in PAT, its corresponding atoms in LST must be the same.
For example:

```
(MATCH '(A B C) '(A B C)) = ((T T))
(MATCH '(A B C) '(A C B)) = NIL
(MATCH '(A 1 C) '(A B C)) = ((1 B) (T T))
(MATCH '(A 1 C 1) '(A B C D)) = NIL
(MATCH '(A 1 C 1) '(A B C B))
                              = ((1 B) (T T))
(MATCH '(A 1 C 2) '(A B C D))
                              = ((1 B) (2 D) (T T))
```

The order of pairs in your answer needn't be the same as above. (Hint:
You may find it helpful to define a help function (MATCH1 PAT
LST PAIRS).)

22. Define (SUBSTITUTE PAT PAIRS), where PAT is a list like
the first argument of MATCH, PAIRS is a list like the ones returned
by MATCH, and SUBSTITUTE returns a list like PAT except every
variable in PAT that is paired with an atom in PAIRS is replaced by
the atom it is paired with. For every appropriate PAT and LST, it
should be the case that (SUBSTITUTE PAT (MATCH PAT
LST)) = LST. (Hint: Use PAIRED-WITH from Exercise 2.8.14.)
Add SUBSTITUTE to your MATCHING file.

2.10 Recursion on S-expressions

We have been treating lists as linear arrangements of unstructured elements. That is, we have been considering both '(A B C) and '((A
B) ((C)) ()) as simply lists of three elements. We now want to
consider the entire structure of lists whose elements are lists. In order to
focus on a concrete example, consider the statement in Exercise 2.9.2, "a
list and its COPY are equal in some sense, but not identical." We would

like to be able to say that `((A B)((C))())` and `((A B)((C))())` are equal as LISP S-expressions, even if they are not identical. We can define precisely what we mean by "equal as LISP S-expressions" by writing a LISP predicate function that takes two S-expressions as arguments and returns T if they are "equal as LISP S-expressions" and NIL otherwise. Remember, we have already written such functions for "equal as lists of atoms" (EQ-LAT of Exercise 2.8.10) and for "equal as sets" (EQUAL-SETS of Exercise 2.9.17). Since this function will be "equal as S-expressions" and every LISP data type is an S-expression, we will simply call it EQUAL.

Let's consider the cases. An S-expression is either an atom or a list. We already have EQ for testing identity of atoms, and atoms have no substructure, so we'll say that two atoms are EQUAL just in case they are EQ. (Some LISPs have different versions of EQ for different kinds of atoms, e.g., INTERLISP's EQP for numbers. We will ignore this for now, and take it up in Exercise 2.10.3.) A list consists of a CAR and a CDR, both of which are S-expressions, so we can say that two lists are EQUAL just in case their CARs are EQUAL and their CDRs are EQUAL. This gives us:

```
(DE EQUAL (S1 S2)
    (COND (if both S1 and S2 are atoms
              then (EQ S1 S2))
          (if both S1 and S2 are lists then
              (EQUAL (CAR S1) (CAR S2))
                      and
              (EQUAL (CDR S1) (CDR S2)))))).
```

EQ can take a non-atom as an argument without giving an error message, but it will surely return NIL if given one atom and one list, so we can simplify our reasoning as follows. If S1 is an atom, it is EQUAL to S2 just in case it is EQ to S2. If S1 is not an atom, but S2 is, they are not EQUAL. If neither is an atom, they are both lists and have CARs and CDRs. If their CARs are EQUAL, S1 and S2 are EQUAL just in case their CDRs are. Otherwise they are not EQUAL. This reasoning gives us:

```
(DE EQUAL (S1 S2)
    (COND ((ATOM S1) (EQ S1 S2))
          ((ATOM S2) NIL)
          ((EQUAL (CAR S1) (CAR S2))
           (EQUAL (CDR S1) (CDR S2)))
          (T NIL))).
```

Will this function always terminate? Recursion takes place on both the CAR and the CDR of both lists. We know that the CDR of a list is one element shorter than the list itself, and we must eventually get to the empty list, NIL. But NIL is an atom! So if either S1 or S2 is the empty list, one of the first two COND pairs will serve as the base case and halt the recursion. What about recursion on the CAR of a list? We can reason this way. According to our first definition of a list from Section 1.4, a list is a left parenthesis followed by zero or more S-expressions followed by a right parenthesis. If we start with a finite list (how could we do otherwise?), it must have a finite number of parenthesis pairs. The CAR of a list will have fewer parenthesis pairs than the list itself. If we keep taking CARs, we will eventually get to a list with one pair of parentheses and no CAR (i.e., NIL), or to an S-expression with no parentheses at all (an atom). In either case we will have an atom, and one of the first two COND pairs will stop us. So we cannot infinitely recurse either on the CDR or on the CAR of a finite list. (Surprisingly, it is possible to create infinite lists in LISP, by using the functions called "destructive list manipulation functions." Don't use any such function until we discuss them later in this book!)

The moral of this discussion is that just as zero is the base case for recursion on integers, and NIL is the base case for recursion on lists, the set of atoms is the base case for recursion on S-expressions. If this is true, can we define non-atomic S-expressions as structures built simply out of atoms, without mention of lists? The answer is yes. We can define S-expressions as follows:

1. Every atom is an S-expression.
2. If S1 and S2 are S-expressions, then (CONS S1 S2) is an S-expression whose CAR is S1 and whose CDR is S2.
3. Nothing else is an S-expression.

Compare this with the definition of lists in Section 1.7. Lists are just special cases of non-atomic S-expressions, such that the CDR of a list is a list or NIL. In general, the result of (CONS S1 S2) is called a *dotted pair*, and is printed as (S1 . S2). Some people stress the idea that the list (A B) is also the dotted pair (A . (B . NIL)), but we will reserve the term "dotted pair" only for those non-atomic S-expressions that cannot be considered lists. As an analogy to the fact that (A . (B . NIL)) is printed as (A B), many LISPs print S-expressions of the form (A . (B . C)) as (A B . C), and refer to these as "dotted lists." We may refer to the normal lists that we are already used to as "strict lists" when the distinction is important. There are also "mixed lists." For example, '(A (B C) . D) is a dotted list whose second element is a strict list. On the other hand, '(A (B . C) D) is a mixed list whose second element is a dotted pair. Dotted pairs were mentioned in Exercise

1.7.2, where we said, "For the time being, if you ever see a dotted pair it will be because you have made a mistake." Now that you know what they are, you still won't use them much. One reason that dotted pairs are less useful than lists is that there is no such thing as an empty, or null, dotted pair. The smallest dotted pair is one whose CAR and CDR are both atoms. The other reason they are less useful is that you cannot evaluate a dotted pair.

We can now again update our collection of S-expressions:

> S-expressions
> > Atoms
> > > Numbers
> > > > Fixed-point
> > > > Floating-point
> > > Literals
> > > Strings
> > Non-atomic S-expressions
> > > Data lists
> > > > Dotted Pairs
> > > > Dotted Lists
> > > > Mixed Lists
> > > > Strict Lists
> > > Forms.

Above, we said that you can only take the CAR of an S-expression a finite number of times. How many times? Let us say that the *depth* of an S-expression is the maximum number of CARs one must take to get to any atom in the S-expression. Equivalently, if you count "1" at the first left parenthesis, increase your count by 1 at each subsequent left parenthesis, and decrease your count by 1 at each right parenthesis, the depth is the maximum your count ever gets (at least if you first replace every "( )" by "NIL"). For example, the depth of '(A (B (C)) (D ((E)) F)) is 4. The most precise definition of "depth" we can give is in LISP:

```
(DEPTH S) EXPR
        Returns the depth—the maximum amount of parenthesis
        nesting of the S-expression, S.
(DE DEPTH (S)
    (COND ((ATOM S) 0); an atom has 0 depth
          (T (ADD1 to the maximum of
                   the depth of the elements
                   of S))))
```

To get the maximum of the depths of the elements of an S-expression, we need to write another function.

```
(MAX-DEPTH-ELTS S) EXPR
        Returns the maximum of depths of the elements of the
        S-expression, S.
(DE MAX-DEPTH-ELTS (S)
   (COND ((ATOM S) 0) ; an atom has no elements
         (T
           (MAX (DEPTH (CAR S))
                (MAX-DEPTH-ELTS (CDR S))))))
```

If MAX is not already defined in our LISP, we have to do that too.

```
(MAX X Y) EXPR
        Returns the greater of the two numbers, X and Y.
(DE MAX (X Y)
   (COND ((GREATERP X Y) X)
         (T Y)))
```

Now let's look at our "program" for finding the depth of an S-expression. It required one main function, one help function probably not useful in its own right, and one utility function certainly useful in its own right.

```
(DE DEPTH (S)
   (COND ((ATOM S) 0)
         (T (ADD1 (MAX-DEPTH-ELTS S)))))
(DE MAX-DEPTH-ELTS (S)
   (COND ((ATOM S) 0)
         (T
           (MAX (DEPTH (CAR S))
                (MAX-DEPTH-ELTS (CDR S))))))
(DE MAX (X Y)
   (COND ((GREATERP X Y) X)
         (T Y)))
```

Notice the interesting recursive structure of DEPTH and MAX-DEPTH-ELTS. They call each other and MAX-DEPTH-ELTS calls itself as well. Also notice that we are treating the empty list as an atom, NIL, and giving it a depth of 0.

Exercises

1. Once more try evaluating (EQ '((A B) ((C)) ()) '((A

B) ((C)) ())). They are not identical, even though they look the same.

2. Define MYEQUAL as given in this section. Try evaluating (MYEQUAL '((A B) ((C)) ()) '((A B) ((C)) ())). They should be EQUAL, even though they are not EQ.

3. Try MYEQUAL with all sorts of S-expressions. Does it work? Try EQ with all sorts of atoms. Does *it* work? If not, for which sorts of atoms does it work and for which doesn't it? Use your manual to find out how to test for equality of other sorts of atoms. Rewrite MYEQUAL so that it works for all sorts of S-expressions.

4. Every LISP has EQUAL already defined. Does your LISP's EQUAL work for every sort of S-expression?

5. Find some destructive list manipulation functions in your manual. Write down their names here:

_____

_____

Don't use them!

6. Play with constructing some dotted pairs. Notice how LISP prints them.

7. Type in '(A . (B . NIL)) and '(A . (B . C)). Notice how LISP prints them.

8. Type in '(A (B C) . D) and '(A (B . C) D). Try to construct both of these by typing nested forms using only CONS and quoted atoms.

9. Ask LISP to evaluate some dotted pairs and dotted lists by typing them to the top level. For example, try (A . B), (CAR . '(A B)), and (CONS 'A . 'B).

10. Define DEPTH (and its auxiliary functions). Test it out on various examples, including lists, dotted pairs, dotted lists, and mixed lists. If the depth of '(A . (B C)) confuses you, remember that '(A . (B C)) = (CONS 'A '(B C)) = '(A B C). You should test a group of functions "bottom up." That is, test MAX before MAX-DEPTH-ELTS before DEPTH. After all, if MAX has a typo in it, DEPTH will certainly not work!

11. Define and test DCOPY, which takes an S-expression and makes a copy of it at all levels. No two corresponding non-atomic elements of an S-expression and its DCOPY, at whatever level, should be EQ, but all should be EQUAL.

12. Define SUBST**. (SUBST** NEW OLD S) should return a copy of S with every sub-expression EQUAL to the S-expression OLD replaced by the S-expression NEW.

13. Define FLATTEN to take a list with an arbitrary nesting of sub-lists and return a list of atoms which have the same left-to-right order as the atoms in the original list. For example, (FLATTEN '(A ((B) (C D) E) (F ((G)))))) should be (A B C D E F G). What is the value of (FLATTEN '(A () B))? The two possible answers are (A B) and (A NIL B). Whichever way your FLATTEN works, write FLATTEN2 to work the other way. They should give the same answers on all lists not containing the empty list as a sub-list.

14. Using RIGHT-MOST, LEFT-ARG, and RIGHT-ARG from your file named COMPUTE (see Exercises 2.8.17, 2.9.19, and 2.9.20), define (PREFIX EXPR) to take a list of numbers separated by "+" and "−", and return the same expression in prefix notation. Make sure that (PREFIX 3) = 3, (PREFIX '(3)) = 3, and (PREFIX '(5 + 2 - 3)) = (- (+ 5 2) 3).

15. Extend your PREFIX function so that it can use the multiplication operator "*" and the division operator "/". For example, (PREFIX '(7 + 12 / 4 - 2 * 3)) should return (- (+ 7 (/ 12 4)) (* 2 3)).

16. Further extend your PREFIX function to allow use of parentheses. For example, (PREFIX '(7 + 12 / (4 - 2) * 3)) should return (+ 7 (* (/ 12 (- 4 2)) 3)), while (PREFIX '((3))) should return 3. Make sure PREFIX does not disturb sub-expressions with no arithmetic operators. For example, (PREFIX '(2 * (SQRT 9.0))) should return (* 2 (SQRT 9.0)). Store this version of PREFIX on COMPUTE.

17. Revise the functions MATCH and SUBSTITUTE on your MATCHING file so that a variable can occur at any level of S-expression nesting.

18. Let a *rule* be a list of two patterns, called the "Left Hand Side" and the "Right Hand Side." Define the functions LHS and RHS so that when given a rule they return the appropriate patterns.

19. Define (APPLY-RULE S RULE), where S is an arbitrary S-expression and RULE is a rule. If (LHS RULE) matches S, APPLY-RULE should return (SUBSTITUTE (RHS RULE) (MATCH (LHS RULE) S)). Otherwise, APPLY-RULE should

return S itself. Test examples like:

```
(APPLY-RULE '(I AM DEPRESSED)
             '((I AM 1) (WHY ARE YOU 1 ?)))
```

Put LHS, RHS, APPLY-RULE, and your revised MATCH and SUBSTITUTE in your MATCHING file.

20. Devise a rule so that (APPLY-RULE '(5 + 2) RULE) = (+ 5 7). Can you use APPLY-RULE to implement PREFIX?

2.11 EVAL

We have said that the difference between a data list and a form is that a form is intended to be evaluated, and therefore must begin with a function name. We have now had practice writing functions which build and return lists. If the list returned by such a function were a form, could we somehow evaluate it? What now happens to such a returned list? Either it is printed on our terminal or it is returned to some function which passes it as an argument to some other function where it is bound to a variable. If LISP prints a form, we can just type it back as the next line. Since what LISP does is evaluate and print the value of every S-expression we type in, this will cause LISP to evaluate a form it has just built. What if a variable inside a function is bound to a form? To evaluate it, we would need to pass it to some evaluator. LISP obviously has such an evaluator, and, marvelously enough, it lets us use it.

I say "marvelously enough" because there is great power in programmers' having the ability to use the evaluator of the programming language they are using. Given that, and the ability to write programs that build source code of that programming language, we can write a program that "writes" and "runs" its own programs! LISP programs (functions) can obviously build LISP source code (the source code just consists of LISP lists), so LISP programmers have this power. We can use it, if we want, to extend LISP into a completely different programming language.

LISP's evaluator is the function EVAL, a SUBR of one argument. It gets its single argument evaluated, and it evaluates it one more time and returns that value. For example:

```
(EVAL 5) = 5
(EVAL A) is an error unless A is bound to
              something that can be evaluated.
(EVAL 'A) is an error unless A is bound.
(EVAL "A) = A
(EVAL (CAR '(A))) is an error unless A is bound.
(EVAL '(CAR '(A))) = A
```

To get an idea of how to use EVAL to extend LISP, let's write a special IF function that's easier to use than COND in certain circumstances. We frequently write simple COND forms looking like

```
(COND (p₁ e₁)
      (T e₂)).
```

For example, MAX was defined in Section 2.10 as

```
(DE MAX (X Y)
  (COND ((GREATERP X Y) X)
        (T Y)))
```

Let's define IF1 so that (IF1 'P 'E1 'E2) returns the value of E1 if P evaluates to a non-null value, and returns the value of E2 if P evaluates to NIL. It will be important that if P is True, E2 should not be evaluated, and if P is False, E1 should not be evaluated.

```
(DE IF1 (P E1 E2)
  (COND ((EVAL P) (EVAL E1))
        (T (EVAL E2))))
```

Using this, we could define MAX as follows:

```
(DE MAX (X Y)
  (IF1 '(GREATERP X Y) 'X 'Y)).
```

When the first EVAL form in IF1 is evaluated, P1 will be bound to the form (GREATERP X Y). EVAL will be given this form and will evaluate it. If it is true, the value of X will be returned. Otherwise, the value of Y will be returned.

The quote marks used in the definition of MAX weren't actually needed, but only because this is a special case. (GREATERP X Y) evaluates to T or NIL, which evaluate to themselves, and numbers also evaluate to themselves. We will see in the exercises that quote marks are usually needed on the arguments of IF1. In the next section, however, we will see how IF1 can be redefined to eliminate the necessity of the quote marks. For another example, let us define a function to build a binary search tree. To see if an element is in a list, MEMBER must search about half the list on average if it succeeds, and all of the list if it fails. Thus, if n elements are on the list, it takes about n operations on the average to search it. A binary search tree, on the other hand, can be searched in about $\log_2(n)$ operations. For now, let us assume we are storing numbers in the tree. An empty binary search tree will be represented by the empty list, NIL. A non-empty binary search tree will be represented by a list of three elements. The first element will be a number that is stored. We will call this "the number at the root of the tree." The second element will be a binary search tree storing all those numbers on the tree less than the number at the root of the tree. The third element will be a binary search tree storing all those numbers on the tree greater or equal to the number at the root of the tree. Notice that the second and/or third elements might be NIL, and will be if only one number is on the tree. Let's see some examples:

> An empty binary search tree: NIL
> Add 5: (5 NIL NIL)
> Add 3: (5 (3 NIL NIL) NIL)
> Add 7: (5 (3 NIL NIL) (7 NIL NIL))
> Add 4: (5 (3 NIL (4 NIL NIL)) (7 NIL NIL))

Now let's define a function to build binary search trees using IF1.

```
(ADD-TO-TREE N TREE) EXPR
        Returns the binary search tree TREE with the number N
        added in the proper place.
    (DE ADD-TO-TREE (N TREE)
      (IF1
        '(NULL TREE)
        '(CONS N '(NIL NIL))
        '(IF1
          '(LESSP N (CAR TREE))
          '(CONS
            (CAR TREE)
            (CONS (ADD-TO-TREE N (CADR TREE))
                  (CONS (CADDR TREE) NIL)))
          '(CONS (CAR TREE)
                 (CONS (CADR TREE)
                       (CONS (ADD-TO-TREE
                                N
                                (CADDR TREE))
                             NIL))))))
```

To search for a number in a binary search tree, compare it with the number in the root. If it is the same, fine. If it is less, look in the first subtree. Otherwise, look in the second subtree.

```
(SEARCHTREE N TREE)
        Returns T if number N is in the binary search tree TREE;
        NIL otherwise.
      (DE SEARCHTREE (N TREE)
        (IF1
          '(NULL TREE)
          'NIL
```

```
                    '(IF1
                     '(EQ N (CAR TREE))
                     'T
                     '(IF1
                        '(LESSP N (CAR TREE))
                        '(SEARCHTREE N (CADR TREE))
                        '(SEARCHTREE N (CADDR TREE))))))))
```

For a final example, consider the function PREFIX you have stored on the file named COMPUTE. The value of (PREFIX '(7 + 12 / 4 – 2 * 3)) is (– (+ 7 (/ 12 4)) (* 2 3)). You should see that it would be easy to change PREFIX so that this value would be (DIFF (PLUS 7 (DIVIDE 12 4)) (TIMES 2 3)). We could then define the function COMPUTE to compute arithmetic expressions written in normal syntax as follows:

(DE COMPUTE (EXPR) (EVAL (PREFIX EXPR))).

The value of (COMPUTE '(7 + 12 / 4 – 2 * 3)) should then be 4.

Exercises

1. Ask LISP to evaluate (CONS 'CAR '('(A))). Then type back to LISP exactly what it types.

2. Have LISP evaluate
   A. (EVAL 5)
   B. (EVAL A)
   C. (EVAL 'A)
   D. (EVAL ''A)
   E. (EVAL (CAR (A)))
   F. (EVAL (CAR '(A)))
   G. (EVAL '(CAR (A)))
   H. (EVAL '(CAR '(A)))
   I. (EVAL (CONS 'CAR '((A))))
   J. (EVAL (CONS 'CAR '('(A))))

3. Define IF1 as in this section.

4. Try (IF1 T ''YES 'ERROR) and (IF1 NIL 'ERROR ''NO). Neither should produce an error. Why are the doubled quotes required?

5. Try (IF1 T 'ERROR ''YES) and (IF1 NIL ''NO 'ERROR). Both should produce errors. Why?

6. Define MYMAX using IF1 and test it.

7. In your LISP, does (MEMBER 'B '(A B C)) return (B C)?

(See Exercises 2.8.7 and 2.8.8.) If so, try (I F1 (MEMBER 'B 'CA B C)) ''YES ''NO). If not, define MYMEMBER as in Exercise 2.8.7 and try (I F1 (MYMEMBER 'B 'CA B C)) ''YES ''NO). Notice that in this case a quote mark on the first argument of I F1 is required.

8. Define ADD-TO-TREE as in this section and test it.

9. Try (ADD-TO-TREE 5 NIL), (ADD-TO-TREE 3 (ADD-TO-TREE 5 NIL)), (ADD-TO-TREE 7 (ADD-TO-TREE 3 (ADD-TO-TREE 5 NIL))), and (ADD-TO-TREE 4 (ADD-TO-TREE 7 (ADD-TO-TREE 3 (ADD-TO-TREE 5 NIL)))).

10. Try (ADD-TO-TREE 4 (ADD-TO-TREE 7 (ADD-TO-TREE 3 (ADD-TO-TREE 5 NIL)))) while tracing ADD-TO-TREE.

11. Define the function (STREEL L) to take a list L of numbers, and build a binary search tree containing all the numbers on L. Don't worry about the order in which the numbers are added to the tree.

12. Define the function SEARCHTREE as in this section, and test it.

13. Redo Exercises 2.5.1–2.5.4 using I F1.

14. Redefine PREF I X on the file COMPUTE so that the list returned uses names of LISP functions instead of symbolic arithmetic operations. To make this easier, define and use the function L I SP-FUN so that, for example, (L I SP-FUN '+) = PLUS.

15. Define COMPUTE as in this section, and store it on the file named COMPUTE.

16. Redo Exercise 1.5.8 using COMPUTE.

17. Redo Exercise 1.6.9 using COMPUTE.

18. Redo Exercise 2.2.12 using COMPUTE. Store D I SCR I M and QUAD-ROOTS on the file COMPUTE.

2.12 FEXPRs

In the last section, we defined COMPUTE so that we could use (COMPUTE '(7 + 12 / 4 - 2 * 3)) instead of (DIFF (PLUS 7 (DIVIDE 12 4))(TIMES 2 3)). This is an improvement, but it would be even better if we could use the form (COMPUTE 7 + 12 / 4 - 2 * 3). There are two problems here. First, this would require COMPUTE to be a function with no fixed number of arguments. (As defined in Section 2.11, COMPUTE is a function of one argument.) Although the form shown here gives COMPUTE nine arguments (COMPUTE is the first element of a ten-element list), we sometimes would want to evaluate something as simple as (COMPUTE 7 + 3), where COMPUTE is given three arguments. All the functions we have defined so far have a fixed number of arguments. The second problem is that COMPUTE, as used here, must not have its arguments evaluated. Although there is no problem evaluating 7 and 12 (they evaluate to themselves), +, /, −, and * are also arguments, and they are not bound to any values. Moreover, we don't want to evaluate them—PREFIX must examine them. Every function we've defined so far gets its arguments evaluated.

We have already discussed and used functions that have arbitrary numbers of arguments and that get their arguments unevaluated. They were special kinds of precompiled functions summarized in Section 2.4. For example, QUOTE is an FSUBR taking one argument unevaluated, while AND is an FSUBR* taking an arbitrary number of arguments unevaluated. The only kind of programmer-defined function we have discussed is an EXPR, which, like a SUBR, takes a fixed number of arguments evaluated. Corresponding to SUBR*, FSUBR, and FSUBR* there is EXPR*, FEXPR, and FEXPR*, programmer-defined functions that take an arbitrary number of arguments evaluated, a fixed number of arguments unevaluated, and an arbitrary number of arguments unevaluated.

Earlier, we said that FSUBRs and FSUBR*s control the evaluation of their arguments themselves. Similarly, FEXPRs and FEXPR*s also control the evaluation of their arguments themselves. Since FEXPRs and FEXPR*s are written by programmers, this requires the programmer to be able to write a form that explicitly evaluates an argument. But we now know how to do this with EVAL! So we're all set.

Functions that take a fixed number of arguments (SUBRs, EXPRs, and FEXPRs) are called *spread* functions, while those that take an arbitrary number of arguments (SUBR*s, EXPR*s, and FEXPR*s) are called *nospread* functions. Nospread functions are defined with only a single lambda variable, but there are two methods of handling that lambda variable. In one method, which we will call the "list of arguments" method, the lambda variable is bound to a *list of the* (evaluated or unevaluated) *arguments*. In the other, which we will call the "number of arguments" method, the lambda variable is bound to the *number of arguments*. In the latter method, a special function is provided to access each of the arguments. Some LISPs use one method, and others use the other. Some LISPs even use one method for EXPR*s and the other for FEXPR*s.

FEXPRs are defined with a list of lambda variables which are bound, in order, to the list of actual arguments when the function is called. The length of the list of lambda variables determines the number of arguments the function must be given. The difference between FEXPRs and EXPRs is that with an EXPR, each lambda variable is bound to the *value* of its corresponding actual argument, while with an FEXPR, each lambda variable is bound to the actual argument itself.

The relationship among EXPRs, EXPR*s, FEXPRs, and FEXPR*s is summarized in Table 2.2. (Compare this with the table in Section 2.5.)

Table 2.2

	Gets arguments evaluated	Gets arguments unevaluated
Fixed number of arguments (spread functions)	EXPR	FEXPR
Arbitrary number of arguments (nospread functions)	EXPR*	FEXPR*

There are a number of ways in which different dialects of LISP differ in their approaches to these four different types of functions. In Table 2.3 there are entries for several dialects of LISP. The columns are: the dialect of LISP, the function type, what that LISP's manual calls the function type, how to define a function of the given type, the method of variable binding for nospread functions. In the column showing how to define a function, "`varlist`" means a list of variables, "`variable`" means a single atomic variable, and "`variables`" means a sequence of variables.

Since ALISP's version is the cleanest, we will continue to use it in this book. In fact, we have added ALISP-like DE and DF to our implementation of Franz LISP.

Now, let's look at some specific examples. An EXPR* takes an arbitrary number of arguments and binds its single lambda variable to a list of the values of these arguments. A simple, but useful EXPR* just returns this list of evaluated arguments. Let's call it L I S T.

(LIST S1 ... Sn) EXPR*

> Takes an arbitrary number of S-expressions and returns a list of their values in order.

(DE LIST ARGS ARGS)

Table 2.3

Dialect	Type	Name	Defining form	Method
ALISP	EXPR	EXPR	(DE fn varlist form)	list
	EXPR*	EXPR*	(DE fn variable form)	
	FEXPR	FEXPR	(DF fn varlist form)	
	FEXPR*	FEXPR*	(DF fn variable form)	list
UCI LISP	EXPR	EXPR	(DE fn varlist form)	num
	EXPR*	LEXPR	(DE fn variable form)	
	FEXPR	---	none	
	FEXPR*	FEXPR	(DF fn (variable) form)	list
Franz LISP	EXPR	LAMBDA	(DEFUN fn varlist form)	num
	EXPR*	LEXPR	(DEFUN fn variable form)	
	FEXPR	---	none	
	FEXPR*	NLAMBDA	(DEFUN fn FEXPR (variable) form)	list
MACLISP	EXPR	EXPR	(DEFUN fn varlist form)	num
	EXPR*	LEXPR	(DEFUN fn variable form)	
	FEXPR	---	none	
	FEXPR*	FEXPR	(DEFUN fn FEXPR (variable) form)	list
INTERLISP	EXPR	EXPR	(DEFINEQ ((fn varlist form)))	num
	EXPR*	EXPR*	(DEFINEQ ((fn (LAMBDA variable form))))	
	FEXPR	FEXPR	(DEFINEQ ((fn (NLAMBDA varlist form))))	
	FEXPR*	FEXPR*	(DEFINEQ ((fn (NLAMBDA variable form))))	list
ZETALISP	EXPR	named-lambda	(DEFUN fn varlist form)	list
	EXPR*	named-lambda	(DEFUN -fn (&REST variable) form)	
	FEXPR	named-lambda	(DEFUN fn (&QUOTE variables) form)	
	FEXPR*	named-lambda	(DEFUN fn FEXPR (variable) form)	list
Common LISP	EXPR	named-lambda	(DEFUN fn varlist form)	list
	EXPR*		(DEFUN fn (&REST variable) form)	
	FEXPR	---	none	
	FEXPR*	---	none	

The first occurrence of "ARGS" is the atomic lambda variable, the second is the form. If we evaluate (LIST 'A 'B 'C), ARGS will be bound to a list of the values of the three arguments—(A B C). Then the form ARGS will be evaluated, and its value will be returned as the value of (LIST 'A 'B 'C). But the value of ARGS is the list (A B C). So (A B C) will be returned as the value of (LIST 'A 'B 'C).

As an example of the number of arguments method of nospread functions, the Franz LISP way of defining LIST is:

> (LIST S1 . . . Sn) LEXPR
>> Takes an arbitrary number of S-expressions and
>> returns a list of their values in order.
> (DEFUN LIST ARGS
>   (LISTIFY ARGS))

In Franz LISP, (LISTIFY n), when used in a LEXPR, returns a list of the first n arguments of the LEXPR. In the same context, (ARG n) returns the nth argument.

In either case, evaluating (LIST 'A 'B 'C) is the same as evaluating (CONS 'A (CONS 'B (CONS 'C NIL))). Similarly, (LIST 'A) is the same as (CONS 'A NIL). LIST is so useful that it is already provided in almost every LISP as a SUBR*.

A good example of an FEXPR is a more convenient version of IF1, defined in Section 2.11. The problem with IF1 was the need to use quotes in forms that used it. The quotes were needed because we wanted only one of the expressions to be evaluated, but IF1, as an EXPR, gets all its arguments evaluated. The quotes delayed evaluation until we wanted it. An FEXPR, however, automatically gets its arguments unevaluated. Let's call the FEXPR version of IF1 IF-ELSE.

> (IF-ELSE P1 E1 E2) FEXPR
>> If P1 evaluates to non-NIL, E1 is evaluated and its value is
>> returned. Otherwise E2 is evaluated and its value is returned.
> (DF IF-ELSE (P1 E1 E2)
>   (COND ((EVAL P1)(EVAL E1))
>   (T (EVAL E2))))

Compare the definition of IF-ELSE to the definition of IF1. The only difference is the IF-ELSE is an FEXPR while IF1 is an EXPR. The difference really shows in their use. Compare the definition of MAX in Section 2.11 using IF1 with this one using IF-ELSE:

```
(DE MAX (X Y)
   (IF-ELSE (GREATERP X Y) X Y)).
```

With FEXPRs and EVAL, we were able to define IF-ELSE, which, in its use, appears to be a fundamental extension of the LISP language. We could even add extra "syntactic sugar" to make an "IF-THEN-ELSE" form:

> (IF P1 THEN E1 ELSE E2) FEXPR
> If P1 evaluates to non-NIL, E1 is evaluated and its value is returned. Otherwise E2 is evaluated and its value is returned. The second and fourth arguments are ignored, but are expected to be the literal atoms THEN and ELSE respectively.

```
(DF IF (P1 THEN E1 ELSE E2)
    (COND ((EVAL P1)(EVAL E1))
          (T (EVAL E2))))
```

Using this IF, we can define MAX as:

```
(DE MAX (X Y)
   (IF (GREATERP X Y) THEN X ELSE Y)).
```

Using DF, we can also explain the predefined LISP function QUOTE by showing how it could be defined as an FEXPR:

```
(DF QUOTE (SEXP) SEXP).
```

Notice that this definition clearly shows that QUOTE takes one argument unevaluated and returns it still unevaluated. Compare this one-line explanation with that in Section 1.8. Not only can we use LISP easily to explain "built-in" LISP functions (and we have been doing this all along), but most of the LISP functions provided in LISP systems were originally programmed in LISP and then compiled. One of the main attractions of LISP as a programming language is that it is so easy for the programmer to extend it to individual taste.

Our example of an FEXPR* is (of course) a better version of COMPUTE. Our new definition is

```
(DF COMPUTE EXPR (EVAL (PREFIX EXPR))).
```

Notice that the only difference between this definition and the previous one is that here COMPUTE is an FEXPR*. EXPR is bound to the list of unevaluated arguments, so when the form (COMPUTE 7 + 12 / 4 − 2 * 3) is evaluated, EXPR is bound to the list (7 + 12 / 4 − 2 * 3) just as it was in the previous version, but the quote mark and extra set of parentheses are no longer needed.

Exercises

1. Define MYLIST as in this section.

2. Evaluate (MYLIST 'A 'B 'C) and (MYLIST 'A).

3. See if your LISP already has LIST defined. If not, add LIST to your file COMPUTE.

4. If your LISP uses the number of arguments method for nospread functions, write its version of (LISTIFY n) here:

   _____

   and its version of (ARG n) here:

   _____

5. Review all your functions on the file COMPUTE. Wherever LIST would be useful, edit the function to use it. In particular, consider PREFIX and QUAD-ROOTS.

6. Define and test IF-ELSE as in this section.

7. Define MAX using IF-ELSE, and test it.

8. Define and test IF as in this section.

9. Redefine MAX to use IF, and test it.

10. See if your LISP already has a function like IF-ELSE or IF.

11. Redo Exercises 2.5.1–2.5.4 using IF-ELSE, IF or your LISP's version of IF.

12. Define MYQUOTE as in this section. Does it work like the predefined QUOTE?

13. Redefine ADD-TO-TREE, STREEL, and SEARCHTREE from Section 2.11 using IF-ELSE, IF, or your LISP's version of IF. Also use LIST where convenient.

14. Define (OLIST TREE) to take a binary search tree and return an ordered list of all the numbers stored in it. (Hint: Contemplate the form (APPEND _____ (CONS _____ _____)) where two of the blanks are filled in with recursive calls to OLIST.)

15. Describe what is done by the MYSTERY function defined as: (DE MYSTERY (L) (OLIST (STREEL L))), where L is a list of numbers.

16. Does your LISP have a function which takes two literal atoms and returns True if the print name of the first is alphabetically before the print name of the second? If so, edit your functions ADD-TO-TREE, STREEL, SEARCHTREE, OLIST, and MYSTERY to get a function that alphabetizes a list of words.

17. Redefine the function COMPUTE on your file named COMPUTE to be as in this section. Test it.

18. Redo Exercises 1.5.8 and 1.6.9 using this version of COMPUTE.

19. Edit the functions DISCRIM and QUAD-ROOTS on the file COMPUTE to use this version of COMPUTE. Test them.

20. Define and test the FEXPR* UNQUOTE, which takes an arbitrary number of S-expressions and returns a list of those S-expressions une-valuated, except that whenever one argument is the atom = and the next argument is some S-expression, the result list will have the value of the S-expression. For example, (UNQUOTE A (ADD1 3) = (SUB1 10) B) will evaluate to the list (A (ADD1 3) 9 B). (HINT: Use a help EXPR for the recursion.)

2.13 Mapping Functions

Occasionally, we want to write a function that takes a list and returns a list just like the old one except that some operation has been performed on every element. For example, consider using a list of numbers to represent a vector, and writing a function to add 1 to every element of the vector. We could do this as follows:

```
(SCALAR-ADD1 VECTOR) EXPR
    VECTOR is a list of numbers.
    Returns a list just like it except each number
    is incremented by 1.

(DE SCALAR-ADD1 (VECTOR)
 (COND
  ((NULL VECTOR) NIL)
  (T (CONS (ADD1 (CAR VECTOR))
           (SCALAR-ADD1 (CDR VECTOR)))))))
```

The only trouble with this definition is it is not clear that the same operation is being performed on every element of the list with no possibility of skipping an element or stopping early. It would be clearer if we could simply say "add 1 to every element." Assume we had a function, APPLY-TO-EACH, that took a function and a list and returned a list of the results of applying the function to each element of the list. If we had, we could define SCALAR-ADD1 as:

```
(DE SCALAR-ADD1 (VECTOR)
   (APPLY-TO-EACH 'ADD1 VECTOR)).
```

That is much clearer! The only problem now is to define APPLY-TO-EACH. Looking at our sample use of it, we see that it takes two arguments, both evaluated, so it must be an EXPR:

```
(APPLY-TO-EACH FN ARGS) EXPR
   FN is a function of one argument.
   ARGS is a list of valid arguments for FN.
   Applies FN to each element of ARGS and
       returns a list of the values.
```

```
(DE APPLY-TO-EACH (FN ARGS)
   (COND
     ((NULL ARGS) NIL)
     (T (CONS (FN (CAR ARGS))
              (APPLY-TO-EACH FN
                             (CDR ARGS))))))
```

Compare this to the function APPLY-1 given in Exercise 2.2.10. Why was COND used to do recursion down the list ARGS when the point seemed to be to avoid this? Couldn't APPLY-TO-EACH be used more directly? Try it, but don't waste too much time!

Although this APPLY-TO-EACH can be used only on functions of one argument, it is not hard to use it on functions of several arguments as long as only one varies. For example, consider the function (SUBST* NEW OLD L) defined in Exercise 2.9.11. Each recursive call is with the CDR of the list L, but NEW and OLD do not change. We can rephrase what SUBST* does as apply to each element of L a function that returns NEW if the element is EQ to OLD, but returns the element itself otherwise. This function takes only one argument, but must use the value of NEW and OLD. We can do this by the direct use of a LAMBDA form (You may want to review Section 2.2):

```
(DE SUBST* (NEW OLD L)
  (APPLY-TO-EACH
    '(LAMBDA (ELT)
        (COND ((EQ OLD ELT) NEW) (T ELT)))
    L))
```

Notice that the LAMBDA form is a function of one argument in which NEW and OLD retain the values they are bound to when SUBST* is called.

Many dialects of LISP already have groups of functions like APPLY-TO-EACH. They are generally called "mapping" functions. (In mathematics, a *map* of one set onto another is a one-to-one correspondence between the elements of each set. APPLY-TO-EACH takes a function and a list and produces another list such that the function forms the correspondence between the elements of the two lists.) The mapping functions most like APPLY-TO-EACH are often called MAPCAR. In some LISPs the arguments are the reverse of what we have done: first the list, then the function. Check with your manual. Mapping functions should be used whenever you could think of applying the same function to every element of a list in parallel.

Exercises

1. Define SCALAR-ADD1 using COND and recursion. Test it.

2. Define APPLY-TO-EACH as shown in this section.

3. Redefine SCALAR-ADD1 using APPLY-TO-EACH. Test it.

4. Define SUBST* as in this section. Test it.

5. Find out if your LISP has a predefined function like APPLY-TO-EACH. If so, redefine SCALAR-ADD1 and SUBST using it.

6. Using our or your LISP's version of APPLY-TO-EACH, define (SCALAR-PLUS N VECTOR) to return the results of adding the number N to every element of the list VECTOR.

7. Using our or your LISP's version of APPLY-TO-EACH, define (SCALAR-TIMES N VECTOR) to return the results of multiplying every element of the list VECTOR by the number N.

8. Define COPY (see Section 2.9) using the techniques of this section. Make sure you check that a copy of a list is EQUAL to, but not EQ to the original.

9. Define the function XPROD of Exercise 2.9.18 using the techniques of this section.

2.14 APPLY

In Section 2.11, we looked at EVAL. It is a SUBR of one argument. It gets its argument evaluated, and evaluates it again. EVAL is the heart of LISP, but it is sometimes inconvenient to use.

Recall that in Section 2.9 we defined (APPEND L1 L2) to return the concatenation of L1 and L2. That is, APPEND returns a list consisting of the members of L1 followed by the members of L2. Consider defining APPEND* as an EXPR* that takes an arbitrary number of lists as arguments, and returns the concatenation of all of them in order. That is, (APPEND*) is NIL, (APPEND* '(A B C)) is (A B C), and (APPEND* '(A B C) '(D E) '(F G H)) is (A B C D E F G H). The plan for writing APPEND* is as follows. Say LISTS is a list of the arguments. If it is empty, return NIL. Otherwise, return the concatenation (using APPEND) of the first list with the concatenation (using APPEND*) of the rest. Let's try this: (Remember, I am using the ALISP-style EXPR* which uses the list of arguments method of variable binding. See Section 2.12.)

(APPEND* L1 ... Ln) EXPR*
    Returns the concatenation of the lists L1, . . . , Ln.

```
        (DE APPEND* LISTS
            (COND ((NULL LISTS) NIL)
                  (T
                   (APPEND (CAR LISTS)
                           (APPEND* (CDR LISTS)))))))
```

That's close, but wrong! The form (APPEND* (CDR LISTS)) calls APPEND* with one argument which is a list of lists, rather than with zero or more arguments each of which is a list. We could, of course, define a help function that takes one list of lists and returns the concatenation of them, but that would be an overabundance of concatenators. What we really want is to evaluate a form with APPEND* as its CAR and the rest of the lists as its CDR. It would seem that we could get this by EVALuating (CONS 'APPEND* (CDR LISTS)). However, there is a slight problem. (CDR LISTS) is not a list of all but the first argument forms originally used in the call to APPEND*, but a list of all but the first actual arguments. If the original call were (APPEND* '(A B C) '(D E) '(F G H)), (CONS 'APPEND* (CDR LISTS)) would be (APPEND* (D E) (F G H)), and EVALing this would require EVALing (D E), which would involve a call to the undefined function

D. Instead, we must quote each element of (CDR LISTS). That is, we must produce a list just like (CDR LISTS), but in which each element L is replaced by 'L (which, remember, is actually the list (QUOTE L)). We can do this by (APPLY-TO-EACH '(LAMBDA (L) (LIST 'QUOTE L)) (CDR LISTS)). So, this version of APPEND* is:

```
(DE APPEND* LISTS
  (COND
   ((NULL LISTS) NIL)
   (T
    (APPEND
     (CAR LISTS)
     (EVAL
     (CONS 'APPEND*
           (APPLY-TO-EACH
            '(LAMBDA (L) (LIST 'QUOTE L))
            (CDR LISTS))))))))).
```

This works, but LISP has a much easier way. Instead of any form like (EVAL (CONS function (APPLY-TO-EACH '(LAMBDA (L) (LIST 'QUOTE L)) arguments))), we can use (APPLY function arguments). APPLY is a SUBR of two arguments. The first is any kind of function. The second is (that is, evaluates to) a list of arguments for the function. APPLY applies the function to the arguments and returns the value. Notice that back in Section 1.5, we said, "The value of a form is the value of the function applied to the arguments." APPLY is LISP's function that applies functions to arguments. (PLUS 5 12) evaluates to 17, as does (APPLY 'PLUS '(5 12)).

Our final version of APPEND*, then, is:

```
(DE APPEND* LISTS
  (COND
   ((NULL LISTS) NIL)
   (T (APPEND
        (CAR LISTS)
        (APPLY 'APPEND* (CDR LISTS)))))).
```

Let's use APPLY to create another useful function. In Section 2.13, we defined (APPLY-TO-EACH FN ARGS) as an EXPR which takes a function of one argument and a list of arguments and returns a list of the results of applying the function to each argument on the list. The fact that FN must be a function of only one argument is a restriction we needn't live with. Consider trying to define the function VECTOR-SUM which takes two lists of the same length and returns another, each element of which is the sum of the two corresponding elements of the original lists. That is, we would want (VECTOR-SUM '(1 2 3) '(4 5 6)) to evaluate to (5 7 9). The way to do VECTOR-SUM is to map PLUS down the two lists in parallel.

To do this, we will define APPLY-TO-EACH* to be an EXPR* which takes one function of *n* arguments (where *n* is at least 1) and *n* lists of arguments each *m* elements long. APPLY-TO-EACH* will return a list of *m* elements, the ith of which is the result of applying the function to a list of arguments each of which is the ith element of its list. Defining APPLY-TO-EACH* will not be as hard as understanding the previous two sentences.

The heart of APPLY-TO-EACH* is forming a list of the CARs of each of a list of lists and applying a function to it. This is just (APPLY function (APPLY-TO-EACH 'CAR list-of-lists)). When you understand that, the rest is easy:

```
(DE APPLY-TO-EACH* ARGS
  (COND
    ((NULL (CADR ARGS)) NIL)
    (T (CONS
         (APPLY
           (CAR ARGS)
           (APPLY-TO-EACH 'CAR (CDR ARGS)))
         (APPLY 'APPLY-TO-EACH*
                (CONS (CAR ARGS)
                      (APPLY-TO-EACH
                       'CDR
                       (CDR ARGS)))))))).
```

Remember that ARGS is bound to the list of evaluated arguments of APPLY-TO-EACH*. Therefore (CAR ARGS) is the function we are applying to lists of arguments and (CDR ARGS) is a list of those lists. Since we require that all these lists be the same size, we can stop as soon as any of them is NULL. (CADR ARGS), being the first, is the easiest to check.

Using APPLY-TO-EACH*, VECTOR-SUM can be defined as follows:

```
(DE VECTOR-SUM (V1 V2)
  (APPLY-TO-EACH* 'PLUS V1 V2)).
```

Since PLUS can take an arbitrary number of arguments, we might want

VECTOR-SUM to do so also. That version would be the EXPR*:

```
(DE VECTOR-SUM VECTORS
   (APPLY 'APPLY-TO-EACH*
          (CONS 'PLUS VECTORS))).
```

Exercises

1. Try evaluating (PLUS 5 12), (EVAL (CONS 'PLUS '(5 12))), and (APPLY 'PLUS '(5 12)).

2. Define APPEND2 to be the two-argument APPEND shown in Section 2.9.

3. Define APPEND* as it was for the first try in this section, but using APPEND2 instead of APPEND. (You may use your IF if you have an appropriate one.) Try it. Note and understand the error message. It may be helpful to trace APPEND* and APPEND2.

4. Edit APPEND* to use (EVAL (CONS 'APPEND* (CDR LISTS))). Test it.

5. Edit APPEND* again, to use EVAL and APPLY-TO-EACH (or your LISP's version). Make sure you understand what is happening in each of these versions.

6. Edit APPEND* again, to use APPLY. Test it.

7. Using the same technique as used in the final version of APPEND*, define MAX* to be a function that takes one or more numbers, and returns the maximum of them.

8. Redefine DEPTH from Section 2.10 to use APPLY, MAX* and APPLY-TO-EACH (or your LISP's version). Test it. Compare it with the Section 2.10 version.

9. Define APPLY-TO-EACH* as shown in this section. Test it. Look in your manual to see if your LISP has a function like it.

10. Define VECTOR-SUM restricted to two arguments. Test it.

11. Redefine VECTOR-SUM so that it takes an arbitrary number of arguments. Test it. Will it work with just one argument? Why or why not?

12. Define VECTOR-PRODUCT like VECTOR-SUM, but using TIMES instead of PLUS.

13. APPLY-TO-EACH* would be even more useful if the lists could be of different lengths. In that case shorter lists would be considered to have their last elements repeated sufficient times to make them equal to the longest. If APPLY-TO-EACH* worked this way, SCALAR-

PLUS of Exercise 2.13.6 could be defined as:

```
(DE SCALAR-PLUS (N VECTOR)
  (APPLY-TO-EACH* 'PLUS (LIST N) VECTOR)).
```

Redefine APPLY-TO-EACH* as suggested here. (Hints: In the first COND pair, stop recursion when the longest argument list has one element in it. In the recursive form, don't take the CDR of a list with only one element in it. In my version, I made use of APPLY-TO-EACH, APPLY, MAX*, LENGTH, and a LAMBDA expression.)

14. Using your improved APPLY-TO-EACH*, define and test SCALAR-PLUS as shown above.

15. Define SCALAR-TIMES using APPLY-TO-EACH*, and test it. (See Exercise 2.13.7.)

16. If we consider VECTOR1 to be a column of n elements, and VECTOR2 to be a row of m elements, the product of the two vectors is a matrix of n rows and m columns whose i^{th} row is each element of VECTOR2 multiplied by the ith element of VECTOR1. A matrix can be represented as a list of rows, each of which is a list. For example, the product of the column (1 2) and the row (3 4 5) would be the matrix ((3 4 5) (6 8 10)). Define (COLUMN-ROW-PRODUCT VECTOR1 VECTOR2) to be the product of the column vector VECTOR1 and the row vector VECTOR2 as described here.

2.15 The FUNARG Problem

What we have been doing in the last two sections is actually dangerous and could cause some subtle errors. I hope that you have not already stumbled across these errors because they can be quite mysterious if you are not prepared for them. In this section, I will try to explain them and suggest some solutions. Other solutions are suggested in the next section.

Recall our definition of APPLY-TO-EACH:

```
(DE APPLY-TO-EACH (FN ARGS)
  (COND ((NULL ARGS) NIL)
        (T (CONS
             (FN (CAR ARGS))
             (APPLY-TO-EACH FN
                            (CDR ARGS)))))).
```

Say we want to define a function that takes a list of integers and a list of arbitrary arguments and returns the list of arguments reordered according to the list of integers. Since such a reordering is called a *permu-*

tation, we will call the function PERM. So (PERM '(2 1 3) '(A B C)) should return (B A C).

We might define PERM as follows:

```
(DE PERM (NUMS ARGS)
  (APPLY-TO-EACH
    '(LAMBDA (N) (NTH N ARGS))
    NUMS)).
```

(See Exercise 2.8.11 for NTH.) If we now try to evaluate (PERM '(2 1) '(A B)), instead of getting (B A), we get (1 1)! We can see the problem by tracing PERM, APPLY-TO-EACH, and NTH. When PERM is called, NUMS is bound to (2 1) and ARGS is bound to (A B). When PERM calls APPLY-TO-EACH, FN is bound to (LAMBDA (N) (NTH N ARGS)) and ARGS is bound to (2 1). Since ARGS is not NIL, the second COND pair is used and the first argument of CONS, (FN (CAR ARGS)) is evaluated. But this is equivalent to ((LAMBDA (N) (NTH N ARGS)) '(2 1)), and since ARGS is now (2 1), this is just (NTH 2 '(2 1)), which is 1. The second time NTH is called, its arguments are 1 and (1), and again it evaluates to 1.

The problem is that when we wrote PERM, we intended "ARGS" in the LAMBDA form to be the second argument of PERM, but when the LAMBDA form was actually applied, it was in the environment of APPLY-TO-EACH, where ARGS was the second argument of APPLY-TO-EACH. The mistake was caused by just happening to use "ARGS" as the second lambda variable of PERM. If we had chosen something else, EXPS say, PERM would have worked!

But it doesn't seem right that whenever we use APPLY-TO-EACH we have to know what its lambda variables are so we can avoid them. We can, instead, draw a more general moral. When we wrote PERM, we passed a function, in this case a lambda expression, as an argument to another function, in this case APPLY-TO-EACH. Whenever we pass a function as an argument, we might have a problem— the FUNARG problem. The problem arises when the function has a *free variable*. A free variable is a variable that will not be bound to a new value when the function is applied to its arguments. In this case ARGS is a free variable since when (LAMBDA (N) (NTH N ARGS)) is applied to its one argument, only N, not ARGS, will be bound to a new value. ARGS will get its value from whatever environment it finds itself in when the form (NTH N ARGS) is evaluated. As we have seen, that environment will be APPLY-TO-EACH's rather than PERM's. The problem is that when we wrote PERM, we intended ARGS to get its value from the environment where we wrote it, but instead it gets its value from the environment where it is evaluated.

We could solve this problem if whenever we pass a function with free variables, we replace all free variables with their proper values.

One way to do this is explicitly with a substitution function. Let (SUBSTITUTE NEW OLD SEXP) return a version of the S-expression SEXP with every occurrence of the atom OLD at any level replaced by the S-expression NEW. Then we could define PERM as:

```
(DE PERM (NUMS ARGS)
  (APPLY-TO-EACH
    (SUBSTITUTE (LIST 'QUOTE ARGS)
                'ARGS
                '(LAMBDA (N) (NTH N ARGS)))
    NUMS)).
```

If you do not understand why we used (LIST 'QUOTE ARGS) instead of just ARGS, see the exercises.

If there were more than one free variable, it would be more convenient if we had a function (SUBSTITUTE-VALUES ATOM-LIST SEXP) which returned a version of the S-expression SEXP with every occurrence of each atom in the list of atoms ATOM-LIST replaced by its value. In that case, we could write PERM as:

```
(DE PERM (NUMS ARGS)
  (APPLY-TO-EACH
    (SUBSTITUTE-VALUES
      '(ARGS)
      '(LAMBDA (N) (NTH N ARGS)))
    NUMS)).
```

Even better would be to have a FEXPR (BIND-FREE-VARIABLES FN) that took either a lambda expression or the name of a function and returned the lambda expression defining the function with all its free variables replaced by their values. In that case, we could write PERM as:

```
(DE PERM (NUMS ARGS)
  (APPLY-TO-EACH
    (BIND-FREE-VARIABLES
      (LAMBDA (N) (NTH N ARGS)))
    NUMS)).
```

Notice that the only difference between this definition of PERM and the first one is that this uses BIND-FREE-VARIABLES where the first used QUOTE. We can consider BIND-FREE-VARIABLES a special kind of QUOTE for use with functional arguments.

SUBSTITUTE-VALUES and BIND-FREE-VARIABLES each

return a function (that can be applied) that has no more free variables. The function is closed off from the influence of the environment in which it is applied. Therefore, such a function is called a *closure*. We will call functions like SUBSTITUTE-VALUES and BIND-FREE-VARIABLES *closure producers*. Some LISPs already have closure producers. UCI LISP, for example, calls it *FUNCTION. *FUNCTION is used like BIND-FREE-VARIABLES, although it does not work exactly like it. Franz LISP has a function, called FCLOSURE, which is used like SUBSTITUTE-VALUES, although it, also, is implemented differently. Franz LISP also has a function called FUNCTION for quoting functions, but which is *not* a closure producer. It acts exactly like QUOTE except when compiling LISP programs. Compiling is beyond the scope of this book, but you should be careful in examining your LISP to distinguish a Franz LISP style FUNCTION from a UCI LISP style *FUNCTION.

Let's try writing SUBSTITUTE-VALUES.

> (SUBSTITUTE-VALUES FREE-LIST SEXP) EXPR
>> Returns a copy of the S-expression SEXP with every occurrence of any atom on FREE-LIST replaced by its value quoted.

```
(DE SUBSTITUTE-VALUES (FREE-LIST SEXP)
  (COND
    ((NULL SEXP) NIL)
    ((ATOM SEXP)
      (COND ((MEMBER SEXP FREE-LIST)
             (LIST 'QUOTE (EVAL SEXP)))
            (T SEXP)))
    (T (CONS
        (SUBSTITUTE-VALUES FREE-LIST
                           (CAR SEXP))
        (SUBSTITUTE-VALUES FREE-LIST
                           (CDR SEXP))))))
```

If we now try (PERM '(2 1) '(A B)) using the version of PERM which uses SUBSTITUTE-VALUES, it will work. But what if we defined SUBSTITUTE-VALUES using ARGS instead of SEXP? In that case (PERM '(2 1) '(A B)) evaluates to (NIL NIL)! The problem here is very similar to the FUNARG problem, and comes from doing an explicit EVAL on an expression (the value of a lambda variable of SUBSTITUTE-VALUES) that was passed into a new environment (from the environment of PERM to that of SUBSTITUTE-VALUES). If you trace APPLY-TO-EACH, you will find that, when it is called in this case, FN is bound to (LAMBDA (N) (NTH N ARGS)). What happened was that when PERM called SUBSTITUTE-VALUES, FREE-LIST was bound to (ARGS) and ARGS was bound to (LAMBDA (N)

(NTH N ARGS)). As SUBSTITUTE-VALUES called itself recursively, FREE-LIST was always bound to (ARGS), but ARGS was bound to the atoms LAMBDA, N, NTH, ARGS, and N again. The only time that the value of ARGS was a MEMBER of FREE-LIST was when its value was ARGS. Its value was then replaced by its value's value (ARGS again), quoted. NTH was called twice, with arguments 2 and ARGS the first time and 1 and ARGS the second time. My version of NTH returns NIL if its second argument is an atom (yours might give an error message). That is why the value of (PERM '(2 1) '(A B)) was (NIL NIL).

Errors of this sort may happen whenever EVAL is called explicitly, and EVAL is most frequently called explicitly in FEXPR and FEXPR*s (see Section 2.12). Therefore some LISPs, such as UCI LISP, have a special mechanism for avoiding these errors. Recall, from Section 2.12, that UCI's FEXPR*, which it calls a FEXPR, is defined with a list of one lambda variable which is bound to the list of unevaluated arguments. For example, to define IF-ELSE in UCI LISP, we would evaluate:

```
(DF IF-ELSE (P-E1-E2)
   (COND ((EVAL (CAR P-E1-E2))
          (EVAL (CADR P-E1-E2)))
         (T (EVAL (CADDR P-E1-E2))))).
```

Such a function can also be defined with two lambda variables. In that case, the second is bound to the environment in effect when the function was called. EVAL, in these LISPs, can be called with a second argument, which must be an environment. EVAL evaluates its argument in this environment instead of the one where EVAL is called. So, in UCI LISP, IF-ELSE could also be defined as:

```
(DF IF-ELSE (P-E1-E2 ENVIRON)
   (COND ((EVAL (CAR P-E1-E2) ENVIRON)
          (EVAL (CADR P-E1-E2) ENVIRON))
         (T
          (EVAL (CADDR P-E1-E2) ENVIRON)))).
```

Having done this, you can call IF-ELSE in the normal way without worrying about the problem we have been describing. The error will not occur! This is *the correct way* to define FEXPR*s that call EVAL in those LISPs that have this feature.

If your LISP has closures, you should always use them when passing functions to functionals (functions that take functions as arguments) that you yourself have written. If your LISP has two-argument FEXPR*s and the two-argument EVAL, you should always use them when defining

FEXPR*s that call EVAL explicitly. If your LISP has *lexical scoping*, like SCHEME or COMMON LISP, you will not have these problems. If your LISP has none of these features, you should define all functionals, FEXPRs, FEXPR*s, and other functions that call EVAL with lambda variables that have strange pnames, which probably won't be used elsewhere, for example, % I F - ELSE - ARG1 %. Your other choice is to use macros, if your LISP has them. Macros are described in the next section.

Exercises

1. Enter the definition of APPLY-TO-EACH as shown in this section. Enter the first definition of PERM, but use EXPS instead of ARGS. Check that PERM works.

2. Edit PERM to use ARGS instead of EXPS. Try evaluating (PERM '(2 1) '(A B)). Trace PERM, APPLY-TO-EACH, and NTH and study the trace until you understand what is happening.

3. Redefine PERM to use SUBSTITUTE. Test (PERM '(2 1) '(A B)). Test this version of PERM both the way it is shown in the text and using just ARGS instead of (LIST 'QUOTE ARGS).

4. Redefine PERM to use SUBSTITUTE-VALUES and define SUBSTITUTE-VALUES as shown in the text. Test (PERM '(2 1) '(A B)).

5. Change SUBSTITUTE-VALUES to use ARGS instead of SEXP and try (PERM '(2 1) '(A B)). PERM and APPLY-TO-EACH should also be using ARGS as a lambda variable. Use the trace facility to study this example until you understand it.

6. Does your LISP have the two-argument FEXPR* and EVAL? If so, redefine SUBSTITUTE-VALUES as such a FEXPR* with ARGS as its only lambda variable, and giving EVAL only one argument. Test PERM this way. It shouldn't work. Then add a second lambda variable to your definition of SUBSTITUTE-VALUES and use it as the second argument to EVAL. PERM should now work properly.

7. Does your LISP have closures? If so redefine PERM to use your closure producer and test it. You may have to redefine APPLY-TO-EACH to use (APPLY FN (LIST (CAR ARGS))) instead of (FN (CAR ARGS)).

2.16 Macros

In the last section, we discussed problems that arise from passing a form into a new environment where some variables in the form have different values than what had been intended. The solution provided by some LISPs is the ability to pass the old environment along with the form. This allows an EVAL in one environment to evaluate a form in another environment.

A different solution is provided by some LISPs in the form of an additional kind of function, called an *execution-time macro*, or simply a *macro*. A macro is a function whose only lambda variable is bound to the entire form (unevaluated) with which it is called. The macro must in turn return a form, called the *macro expansion*, which is then evaluated. The value of the macro expansion is then returned as the value of the original form. The significant point is that the macro expansion is evaluated *outside* the environment of the macro's definition, and *in* the environment of the original macro call. Our version of Franz LISP has macros which can be defined in any of the following ways:

```
(DEF fn (MACRO (var) body))
(DEFUN fn MACRO (var) body)
(DM fn (var) body).
```

The first is Franz LISP's basic way of defining macros. DEFUN and DM are actually themselves macros which make it easier to define other macros. We will see later how to define them. I will use DM since it involves the least typing.

In any case, the name of the macro being defined is f n, the one lambda variable is var, and body is a form. When LISP evaluates a form whose CAR is f n, it saves the current value of var, binds var to the form, evaluates body getting the macro expansion, restores the saved value of var, and evaluates the macro expansion, returning this value as the value of the original form. As a simple case, let's define F I RST to be equivalent to CAR:

```
(DM FIRST (FORM) (CONS 'CAR (CDR FORM))).
```

If we now evaluate (FIRST '(A B C)), FORM will be bound to (FIRST '(A B C)). Then (CONS 'CAR (CDR FORM)) will be evaluated giving (CAR '(A B C)). After restoring FORM's old value, this will be evaluated to A, which will be returned as the value of (FIRST '(A B C)).

Let's try evaluating (SECOND '(A B C)) where SECOND is an EXPR defined by:

```
(DE SECOND (FORM) (FIRST (CDR FORM)).
```

This may look like it will give us problems, but it won't. First FORM is bound to (A B C) and (FIRST (CDR FORM)) is evaluated. The old value of FORM is saved, and FORM is bound to (FIRST (CDR FORM)). (CONS 'CAR (CDR FORM)) is evaluated giving (CAR

⟨CDR FORM⟩⟩. The previous value of FORM, namely ⟨A B C⟩, is restored, and ⟨CAR ⟨CDR FORM⟩⟩ is evaluated, giving B. This is returned as the value of ⟨FIRST ⟨CDR FORM⟩⟩ and as the value of ⟨SECOND '⟨A B C⟩⟩. It worked because the last evaluation was done outside the environment of the macro definition.

Now let's try defining IF-ELSE as a macro. Instead of having a COND calling EVAL inside the definition, we will have the macro expand to a COND to be evaluated outside of the macro definition. We will transform the IF-ELSE form into an equivalent COND. That is, we will transform ⟨IF-ELSE P E1 E2⟩ into ⟨COND ⟨P E1⟩ ⟨T E2⟩⟩. So, the definition is:

```
(DM IF-ELSE (F-P-E1-E2)
   (LIST 'COND
         (LIST (CADR F-P-E1-E2)
               (CADDR F-P-E1-E2))
         (LIST 'T (CADDDR F-P-E1-E2)))).
```

To make this easier to read, let's use NTH and the SUBSTITUTE function used briefly in the previous section:

```
(DM IF-ELSE (F-P-E1-E2)
   (SUBSTITUTE
      (NTH 2 F-P-E1-E2)
      'P
      (SUBSTITUTE
         (NTH 3 F-P-E1-E2)
         'E1
         (SUBSTITUTE
            (NTH 4 F-P-E1-E2)
            'E2
            '(COND ((P E1) (T E2))))))).
```

Notice that this definition simply substitutes the correct arguments into a pattern of the form we want.

Two additional facilities, supported by several LISPs, make this even easier. First, an S-expression preceded by a backquote (ʻ) evaluates to itself except that every S-expression within it preceded by a comma is replaced by its value. (Compare the function UNQUOTE from Exercise 2.12.20.) Thus, if P is bound to the list ⟨GREATERP X Y⟩, E1 is bound to X, and E2 to Y, ʻ⟨COND ⟨,P ,E1⟩ ⟨T ,E2⟩⟩ evaluates to ⟨COND ⟨⟨GREATERP X Y⟩ X⟩ ⟨T Y⟩⟩. If the comma is immediately followed by "@", then the value of the next S-expression is "spliced" into the current list. For example, if ARGS is bound to the list (X Y), then

```
'(COND ((GREATERP ,@ARGS) ,(CAR ARGS))
       (T ,(CADR ARGS)))
```

evaluates to (COND ((GREATERP X Y) X) (T Y)).

Second, if a macro is to be defined with a fixed number of arguments, these LISPs allow it to be defined as (DEFMACRO fn (var$_1$ . . . var$_n$) body). In this case, as in a FEXPR, var$_i$ is bound to the unevaluated i^{th} argument of the macro. So, finally, we could define IF-ELSE as:

```
(DEFMACRO IF-ELSE (P E1 E2)
  '(COND (,P ,E1) (T ,E2))).
```

Compare this with the definition of IF-ELSE in Section 2.12. This macro definition is both simpler and safer!

Unfortunately, not every LISP has macros, but if you use one that does, always use macros instead of FEXPRs with explicit calls to EVAL.

A common use of macros is to extend a function of two arguments into one of an arbitrary number of arguments. In Section 2.14, we used APPLY to extend a two-argument APPEND into an arbitrary number of arguments APPEND*. Here we will do it using macros. The plan is as follows: If APPEND* has no arguments, NIL is the answer; otherwise APPEND* can be applied to all arguments but the first, and APPEND can be applied to the first argument and the result returned by APPEND*. This is the same plan we used in Section 2.14, but using macros it is easy to follow:

```
(DM APPEND* (ARGS)
   (COND ((NULL (CDR ARGS)) NIL)
         (T '(APPEND
              ,(CADR ARGS)
              (APPEND* ,@(CDDR ARGS))))))).
```

Remember that ARGS will be bound to a form such as (APPEND* '(A B C) '(D E) '(F G H)), (CAR ARGS) will be AP-PEND*, and (CDR ARGS) will be the list of unevaluated arguments ('(A B C) '(D E) '(F G H)). The first macro expansion will be (APPEND '(A B C) (APPEND* '(D E) '(F G H))). To evaluate this, APPEND* will be called again. Finally, the full macro expansion will be (APPEND '(A B C) (APPEND '(D E) (APPEND '(F G H) NIL))). This will then be evaluated to (A B C D E F G H).

Finally, we said that DEFUN and DM were themselves macros. We will show the definition of DEFUN here, and leave DM for you to do as an exercise. Remember, we have to use DEF to define DEFUN. We will use DFMVB as the lambda variable to remind us of the five elements of a DEFUN form.

```
(DEF DEFUN
   (MACRO (DFMVB)
      '(DEF ,(CADR DFMVB) ,(CDDR DFMVB))))
```

Exercises

1. Does your LISP have execution-time macros? If not, proceed on to the next section, but remember to be careful when defining FEXPRs, calling EVAL, and passing functions as arguments. Write your LISP's version of (DM fn (var) body) here:

_____.

2. Franz LISP has a function (MACROEXPAND FORM), which returns the macro expansion of FORM, so you can check it. If your LISP has such a function, write its name here:

_____.

3. Define FIRST as a macro. Have LISP show you the macro expansion of (FIRST '(A B C)). Evaluate (FIRST '(A B C)) while tracing FIRST and CAR.

4. Define SECOND as shown in this section. Look at the macro expansion of (SECOND '(A B C)). See if (SECOND '(A B C)) really works. Look at the macro expansion of (SECOND (FIRST (SECOND '(A ((B C) D))))) and evaluate it while tracing FIRST and SECOND.

5. Define IF-ELSE as a macro using any of the methods of this section.

6. Define MAX using this version of IF-ELSE, and test it.

7. Does your LISP have the backquote (`), comma (,), and at sign (@) features? If not, redefine UNQUOTE from Exercise 2.12.20 to include @ and use it instead.

8. Actually the backquote (`), comma (,), and at sign (@) are special characters called _read-time macros_. When you type them into LISP they are immediately replaced by something else. Nevertheless, what was said in this section about their effect is true. If your LISP has such characters, see how they work by typing the following lines and study what LISP types back:

```
'`(A ,ARGS)
'`(A ,ARGS B)
```

```
'`(A ,@ARGS B)
'`(A ,@ARGS)
'`,ARGS
'`(COND (,P ,E1) (T ,E2))
'`(COND ((GREATERP ,@ARGS) ,(CAR ARGS))
         (T ,(CADR ARGS))).
```

9. Define APPEND* as shown in this section and test it. Look at the macro expansion of (APPEND* '(A B C) '(D E) '(F G H)). Use IF-ELSE instead of COND in the definition of APPEND*.

10. Define MAX* using the techniques of this section. (See Exercise 2.14.7.)

11. We introduced LISP's AND in Section 2.4 AND evaluates its arguments left to right and returns NIL as soon as one of its arguments evaluates to NIL. If all arguments evaluate to non-NULL values, AND returns the value of its last argument. Define a macro, MYAND, that works like AND. Test it by looking at the macro expansion of (MYAND (ZEROP (PLUS 5 -5)) (ZEROP (PLUS 5 -3)) (ZEROP (PLUS 3 -5))) and evaluating it while tracing MYAND, ZEROP and PLUS. Did your MYAND evaluate only the first two arguments?

12. We also saw in Section 2.4 that the function OR is like AND, but returns NIL only if all its arguments evaluate to NIL. Otherwise, it returns the value of the first argument whose value is not NIL. Write a macro, MYOR, that works like OR. Test it by looking at the macro expansion of (MYOR (ZEROP (PLUS 5 −3)) (ZEROP (PLUS 5 -5)) (ZEROP (PLUS 3 -5))) and by evaluating it while tracing MYOR, ZEROP and PLUS. Check that the third argument is not evaluated. Is the second argument evaluated only once? If not, redefine MYOR so that no argument is evaluated more than once. (Hint: Compare (COND ((NULL S1) S2) (T S1)) with ((LAMBDA (S) (COND ((NULL S) S2) (T S))) S1).)

13. Define DEFUN as shown in this section and test it.

14. Define DM as a macro and test it.

15. If you have not done so already, define IF-ELSE using DEFMACRO as shown in this section. (If your LISP has it.) Look at the stored definition of IF-ELSE. Notice that DEFMACRO is itself a macro that defines IF-ELSE as if it took an arbitrary number of arguments.

16. Define DEFMACRO yourself and test it. Hint: If your LISP doesn't already have DEFMACRO, here is what mine printed for the previous exercise:

```
(DEF IF-ELSE
   (MACRO (DEFMACROARG)
             ((LAMBDA (P E1 E2)
                      (LIST
                         'COND
                         (LIST P E1)
                         (LIST 'T E2)))
                 (CADR DEFMACROARG)
                 (CADDR DEFMACROARG)
                 (CADDDR DEFMACROARG)))).
```

17. Edit your file COMPUTE, to use macros instead of explicit calls to EVAL. Make sure everything still works.

Chapter 3

Programming in Non-Applicative LISP

3.1 SET and SETQ

Up to now, everything we have done with LISP has been using what is called "pure" LISP. That is, with a few minor exceptions, using LISP as a pure *applicative* (or *functional*) programming language. An applicative programming language is one in which the only thing one can do is *apply* functions to their arguments and get back their values. When that happens, the environment of the programming system has not changed. After evaluating (CONS 'A (CDR '(X B C))), everything is the same as it would have been had we not done it. As we saw in Section 2.15, the environment of one evaluation may differ from the environment of an embedded evaluation, but when we return to the top level, nothing has changed. The exceptions are: 1) after defining a function, the environment has changed in that a new function is defined; 2) after editing a function the environment has changed in that the function has a different definition; 3) after saving definitions on a file, or loading them from a file; 4) after turning tracing on or off. Changing the environment is called *side-effecting*. Functions like DE are used principally for their side-effects rather than for their values. Although applicative programming has started becoming more popular recently, LISP, or rather the pure subset of LISP, was the first applicative programming language.

Even though any program that can be written in any programming language can be written in pure LISP, LISPers often find the non-pure facilities of LISP helpful. They are the subject of the remaining sections of this book.

The most basic non-pure (or side-effecting) functions in LISP are SET and SETQ. As you recall from Section 1.3, most literal atoms have no value at the top level of LISP. They get values when they are lambda variables of a function and the function is applied to some arguments. SET and SETQ are alternative ways of giving a literal atom a value. They are like the assignment statement in non-applicative programming languages.

SET is a SUBR of two arguments. The value of the first argument must be a literal atom. The value of the second can be any S-expression. SET returns the value of its second argument, but its major purpose is making the value of the value of its first argument be the value of its second argument. For example, if you type (SET 'X (PLUS 5 3)) to LISP, LISP will type back 8, but, more important, the value of X will now be 8. So, if you now type X to LISP, instead of giving an error message, LISP will type back 8.

(SETQ X Y) is exactly equivalent to (SET 'X Y), but is much more frequently used. If you use a non-applicative language, you will recognize (SETQ X Y) as the LISP version of the assignment statement X := Y (or X = Y).

The effect SET and SETQ have is on whatever environment they are evaluated in. If done at top-level LISP, the atom is given a value at top level, which is saved whenever it is bound as a lambda variable, and restored when the function exits. If done in an environment in which the atom is a lambda variable, the new value is in effect only until the value of the higher environment is restored.

As an example of using SETQ on a lambda variable, consider writing a macro or FEXPR that takes two arguments, returns the value of the first if it is not NIL, and returns the value of the second otherwise. This was part of Exercise 2.16.12, and is a two-argument OR, so we will call it OR2. The macro version could be written as:

```
(DEFMACRO OR2 (S1 S2)
  '(COND  (,S1 ,S1) (T ,S2)))
```

and the FEXPR version could be written as:

```
(DF OR2 (%S1% %S2%)
   (COND ((EVAL %S1%) (EVAL %S1%))
         (T (EVAL %S2%)))).
```

The trouble with these versions is that if the first argument does not evaluate to NIL, it is evaluated twice. One solution hinted at in Exercise 2.16.12 is to use a lambda expression, as:

```
'(DEFMACRO OR2 (S1 S2)
   '((LAMBDA (S) (COND (S S) (T ,S2)))
     ,S1)).
```

(The FEXPR version is left as an exercise.) This is a good pure LISP solution to the problem. A solution using SETQ would be:

```
(DF OR2 (%S1% %S2%)
   (COND ((SETQ %S1% (EVAL %S1%)) %S1%)
         (T (EVAL %S2%)))).
```

(Here, the macro version is left as an exercise.) Notice what happens: %S1% is first bound to the unevaluated first argument; it is evaluated by EVAL, and changed by SETQ so that %S1% is now bound to the value of the first argument of OR2; this value is tested by COND, since SETQ returns the value of its second argument; if it is not NIL, COND returns the value of %S1%, which, by now, is the value of OR2's first argument. When OR2 returns, %S1% and %S2% are restored to the status they had before OR2 was called.

Exercises

1. Try typing the atom X to LISP. Does it have a value?

2. Evaluate (SET 'X (PLUS 5 3)). What value does SET return? What value does X have now?

3. Evaluate (SETQ X 'Y). What value does X have now?

4. Evaluate (SET X (PLUS 9 2)). What value does X have now? What value does Y have now?

5. What is the value of (EVAL X)? Why?

6. Do several parts of Exercise 1.7.5 again. Now do (SETQ L '(((A B) (C D) E) (F G) (H) I)). Now redo Exercise 1.7.5 by typing in forms such as (CDAR L) and (CDDAR L). After each one, check that the top-level value of L hasn't changed.

7. Define OR2 as a macro or FEXPR using the first version. Check the top-level value of S1 (or %S1%). Make the top-level value of Y be '(A). Evaluate (OR2 (CAR Y) (CDR Y)) while tracing OR2 and CAR. Notice the double evaluation of (CAR '(A)). Recheck the top-level value of S1.

8. Redefine OR2 using the lambda expression. Rerun the tests of Exercise 7.

9. Redefine OR2 using SETQ. Again rerun the tests of Exercise 7.

10. Reread Exercise 2.10.19. There we said, "If (LHS RULE) matches S, APPLY-RULE should return (SUBSTITUTE (RHS RULE) (MATCH (LHS RULE) S)). Otherwise, APPLY-RULE should return S itself." If you wrote APPLY-RULE exactly as described,

you would have written

```
(DE APPLY-RULE (S RULE)
  (COND ((MATCH (LHS RULE) S)
         (SUBSTITUTE
          (RHS RULE)
          (MATCH (LHS RULE) S)))
        (T S))).
```

The problem with this version is that if (MATCH (LHS RULE) S) succeeds, it is evaluated twice, and it may be a long, expensive operation. A better way to have written it would be

```
(DE APPLY-RULE (S RULE)
  ((LAMBDA (LP)
     (COND (LP (SUBSTITUTE (RHS RULE) LP))
           (T S)))
   (MATCH (LHS RULE) S))).
```

However, as we showed for OR2, some people are tempted to use SETQ to avoid the double evaluation. Here, though, we cannot afford to change either lambda variable to the value of the call of MATCH. (Why not?) So, some people use a new variable, as in:

```
(DE APPLY-RULE (S RULE)
  (COND ((SETQ LP (MATCH (LHS RULE) S))
         (SUBSTITUTE (RHS RULE) LP))
        (T S))).
```

Load your MATCHING file, and temporarily edit your version of APPLY-RULE so it looks like this last version. Make the top-level value of LP be '((1 THINKS I AM 2) (DO YOU THINK YOU ARE 2)), and then evaluate (APPLY-RULE '(MOTHER THINKS I AM LAZY) LP). Now what is the top level of LP? We say that APPLY-RULE has *side-effected a global variable*. This was because APPLY-RULE changed the value of a free variable (one that wasn't one of APPLY-RULE's lambda variables). This can be very dangerous and is one of the negative features of non-applicative programming.

11. To appreciate the dangers of side-effecting global variables, define the function:

> (APPLY-RULES S LP) EXPR
> > S is an S-expression,
> > and LP is a list of rules (pairs of patterns). APPLY-RULES

transforms S by applying each rule in LP successively, and
returns the results.

```
(DE APPLY-RULES (S LP)
   (COND ((NULL LP) S)
         (T (APPLY-RULES
               (APPLY-RULE S (CAR LP))
               (CDR LP)))))
```

Set the top-level value of RULES as:

```
(SETQ RULES
    '(((JOHN 1 2) ((N JOHN) 1 2))
      ((1 LOVES 2) (1 (V LOVES) 2))
      ((1 2 MARY) (1 2 (N MARY)))
      ((1 (V 2) (N 3))
       (1 (VP (V 2) (N 3))))
      (((N 1) (VP 2 3))
       (S (N 1) (VP 2 3)))))
```

and test (APPLY-RULES '(JOHN LOVES MARY) RULES).
If this results in an error, look at the value of LP while you are in the
break package. If you still don't understand what is happening, test it
again while tracing APPLY-RULES and APPLY-RULE.

12. Rewrite APPLY-RULE according to the "better way" shown above,
and test (APPLY-RULES '(JOHN LOVES MARY) RULES)
again. You have written a small, admittedly inflexible, parser of a tiny
fragment of English. Save this version of APPLY-RULE and this
APPLY-RULES on your MATCHING file.

13. Some LISPs allow SET and SETQ to have any even number of arguments. Each odd-numbered argument is given as its new value the
value of the following even-numbered argument. This is done in order
from left to right. See if your LISP allows this by evaluating (SETQ
X 3 Y 5 Z (PLUS X Y) Y 33) and then looking at the values of X, Y, and Z.

3.2 Sequences

One way in which I have told less than the whole truth (for good peda-
gogical reasons) in the discussion of LISP so far concerns the topic of
sequences of forms. For example, in Section 2.1, I said that the function
DE takes three arguments—a function name, a list of variables, and a
form, and, in general, I have said that the body of every kind of function
(FEXPR, MACRO, etc.) consists of a single form. In fact, in most modern

LISPs, that is not true. In general, the body of a function can be a sequence of one or more forms. When the function is called, after the binding of the variables, the sequence of forms is evaluated one after the other in order. The value of the last form in the sequence is the value returned by the function call. The values of the previous forms in the sequence are ignored. If the sequence consists of just one form, then what I have previously said about function evaluation still holds.

So let's consider the general format of DE:

$$\texttt{(DE fn varlist form}_1 \ . \ . \ . \ \texttt{form}_{n-1} \ \texttt{form}_n \texttt{)}.$$

When fn is called, the current values of the variables are saved, the variables are bound to the values of the actual arguments, $\texttt{form}_1$ through $\texttt{form}_n$ are evaluated, the old values of the variables are restored, and the value of $\texttt{form}_n$ is returned. If the values of $\texttt{form}_1$ through $\texttt{form}_{n-1}$ are ignored, what good are they? If we are restricting ourselves to pure, applicative LISP, they are of *no* good, which is why I have not mentioned this possibility until now. However, if $\texttt{form}_1$ through $\texttt{form}_{n-1}$ cause side-effects, then these side-effects will, indeed, occur. For example, another way to define the version of APPLY-RULE used in Exercise 3.1.10 is:

```
(DE APPLY-RULE (S RULE)
   (SETQ LP (MATCH (LHS RULE) S))
   (COND (LP (SUBSTITUTE (RHS RULE) LP))
         (T S))).
```

The first form has the effect of setting the value of LP to the value returned by MATCH. Then the COND is evaluated, and its value is returned. MATCH is called only once regardless of what its value is.

Another place where sequences are allowed is in COND. In Section 2.5, I said that the form of a COND is $\texttt{(COND (p}_1 \ \texttt{e}_1\texttt{)} \ . \ . \ . \ \texttt{(p}_n \ \texttt{e}_n\texttt{))}$. Actually, in most LISPs each $\texttt{e}_1$ can be a sequence of zero or more S-expressions. That is, each COND "pair" is a list of one or more S-expressions. So, let's change terminology, and say COND *clause*, instead of COND pair. If the first S-expression of a clause evaluates to NIL, the next clause is considered. If the first S-expression of a clause evaluates to any non-NIL value, the rest of the S-expressions of that clause are evaluated in order, and the value of the last one is returned as the value of the COND. Values of earlier S-expressions in the clause are ignored—they are evaluated for effect only.

Earlier dialects of LISP did not allow sequences as we have been discussing them. To make up for it, they had a special FSUBR* called PROGN. The form of a PROGN is $\texttt{(PROGN form}_1 \ . \ . \ . \ \texttt{form}_n\texttt{)}$. The $\texttt{form}_i$ are evaluated in order and the value of the last one is returned as the value of the PROGN. Many modern LISPs retain PROGN, although the existence of sequences removes most need of it.

In general, a LISP form returns the value of the last S-expression actually evaluated within it, but there are exceptions. For example, Franz LISP has PROG1, which is like PROGN, but after all $form_1$ are evaluated, the value of the first is returned. It also has PROG2, which is like PROGN except the value of the second argument is returned.

Exercises

1. Does your LISP allow sequences of forms in function definitions? If so, define and test this section's version of APPLY-RULE.

2. Does your LISP allow generalized COND clauses? If so, first give X and Y the top-level values of ORIGX and ORIGY, respectively, and then evaluate

```
(COND ((NULL X))
      ((ATOM Y) (SETQ Y (LIST Y)) 'DONE))
      (Y)).
```

What was its value? What is the value of X and Y now? Evaluate the same COND again. What is its value now?

3. The meaning of a COND clause with only one S-expression is "if this S-expression evaluates to non-NIL, return its value," and it is not re-evaluated. To see the benefit of this, define OR2 as:

```
(DEFMACRO OR2 (S1 S2)
  `(COND (,S1) (,S2))).
```

Compare this with the definition in Section 3.1, and redo Exercise 3.1.7.

4. Does your LISP have PROGN? If not, define it yourself as a macro, FEXPR, or EXPR*. Even if it does, define MYPROGN to act just like PROGN. Test it by evaluating (MYPROGN (SETQ X 'A) (SETQ X 'B) (SETQ X 'C)) and seeing what value X has afterward.

5. Does your LISP have PROG1 and PROG2? If not, define them. If so, define MYPROG1 and/or MYPROG2. Test them with the same sequence of forms used for Exercise 4.

6. Define NPROG as a function that takes at least two arguments, the first of which evaluates to an integer, n. The function should evaluate all its arguments, and return the value of the $n+1^{st}$. For example, (NPROG 2 s_1 . . . s_n) should do exactly what (PROG2 s_1 . . . s_n) does.

7. Give the variable STACK the top-level value NIL. Then define two side-effecting functions (PUSH S) and (POP). (PUSH S) should CONS the value of S onto the front of STACK, and return the value of S. (POP) should return the CAR of STACK, and change STACK to be its CDR. Be sure PUSH doesn't cause S to be evaluated more than once. Table 3.1 should clarify what is wanted.

Table 3.1

Form	Value of form	Value of STACK
		( )
(PUSH 23)	23	(23)
(PUSH 40)	40	(40 23)
(POP)	40	(23)
(POP)	23	( )

8. One reason that the parsing rules you used in Exercises 3.1.11-3.1.12 were so inflexible is that variables can match only a single S-expression. But suppose we had a different class of variables, that could match sequences of 0 or more S-expressions. If X and Y were such variables, the pattern (X LOVES Y) would match all of the S-expressions, (JOHN LOVES MARY), (JOHN LOVES THE GIRL WHO LIVES DOWN THE STREET FROM HIM), and (JOHN LOVES). In each case, X would be paired with the sequence (JOHN), but Y would be paired with the sequences, (MARY), (THE GIRL WHO LIVES DOWN THE STREET FROM HIM), and (). Let us call such variables *sequence variables*. Add to your MATCHING file the function (SVARIABLEP V), which returns True if V is a sequence variable and NIL if it is not. Initially, make the atoms X, Y, and Z the only sequence variables.

9. I assume you have in your MATCHING file a recursive function like (MATCH1 PAT SEXP PAIRS) that does all the work. Add in the appropriate place the COND clause,

```
((SVARIABLEP (CAR PAT))
   (BACKTRACK-MATCH (CAR PAT)
                    (CDR PAT)
                    SEXP
                    NIL
                    PAIRS)),
```

and define the function:

```
(DE BACKTRACK-MATCH
   (V PAT SEXP SQCE PAIRS)
   (COND
     ((NULL PAT)
      (CONS (LIST V (APPEND SQCE SEXP))
            PAIRS))
     ((MATCH1 PAT
              SEXP
              (CONS (LIST V SQCE) PAIRS)))
     ((NULL SEXP) NIL)
     (T (BACKTRACK-MATCH
          V
          PAT
          (CDR SEXP)
          (APPEND SQCE (LIST (CAR SEXP)))
          PAIRS)))).
```

The call of BACKTRACK-MATCH from MATCH1 tries to match the sequence variable with NIL, and the rest of the PAT with the rest of the S-expression. BACKTRACK-MATCH is a *backtracking* function whose four COND clauses do the following:

A. If there is no more pattern, the sequence variable matches the sequence built up so far appended to the rest of the S-expression.
B. If, assuming the sequence variable matches the sequence built up so far, the rest of the pattern matches the rest of the S-expression, that match is the match to be returned. Notice the use of a single form in the COND clause.
C. Otherwise, if there is no more S-expression, there is no match.
D. But if there is more S-expression, given that the current sequence didn't work out, try extending the sequence one more sub-S-expression.

BACKTRACK-MATCH is called a backtracking function, because if, in the second COND clause, the currently proposed sequence doesn't work out, we *backtrack* to this recursive level and try a different sequence.

10. Trace BACKTRACK-MATCH while evaluating (MATCH '(X C) '(A B C)).

11. Try:

    (MATCH '(X LOVES Y) '(JOHN LOVES MARY)).

```
(MATCH '(X LOVES Y)
        (JOHN LOVES THE GIRL WHO LIVES
                DOWN THE STREET FROM HIM)),
```
and `(MATCH '(X LOVES Y) (JOHN LOVES))`.

12. Redefine the version of SUBSTITUTE on your MATCHING file, so it can use sequence variables.

13. Make sure `(MATCH '(X B X) '(A B C B A B C))` works, and pairs X with the sequence `(A B C)`.

14. Redo Exercise 3.1.12 with the following set of rules:

```
(SETQ RULES
  '((((X JOHN Y) (X (N JOHN) Y))
    ((X LOVES Y) (X (V LOVES) Y))
    ((X MARY Y) (X (N MARY) Y))
    ((X (V Y) (N Z)) (X (VP (V Y) (N Z))))
    ((X (V Y)) (X (VP (V Y))))
    (((N X) (VP Y)) (S (N X) (VP Y))))))
```

Also try `(APPLY-RULES '(MARY LOVES JOHN) RULES)` and `(APPLY-RULES '(JOHN LOVES) RULES)`. Make sure all your modifications to your MATCHING file are stored there for later use.

3.3 Local Variables

In Exercises 3.1.10 and 3.1.11, we saw a free variable used in a function definition. When its value was changed by SETQ, this change had unforeseen effects on outer environments. Some LISPs have special-purpose FSUBR*s for introducing new, non-lambda variables inside their own environments. Franz LISP and MACLISP call this FSUBR* LET. Remember the function definition we are discussing:

```
(DE APPLY-RULE (S RULE)
  (COND ((SETQ LP (MATCH (LHS RULE) S))
          (SUBSTITUTE (RHS RULE) LP))
        (T S))).
```

The SETQ changes the value of LP in the innermost dynamically containing environment in which it is a lambda variable, or, if none, at the top level. However, using LET, we can define APPLY-RULE as:

```
(DE APPLY-RULE (S RULE)
   (LET (LP)
        (COND ((SETQ LP
                     (MATCH (LHS RULE) S))
               (SUBSTITUTE (RHS RULE) LP))
              (T S)))).
```

The effect of the LET is to set up a new environment for LP. Now the change to LP does not affect any outer environment.

The format for LET forms is somewhat like that of LAMBDA forms: (LET varlist form$_1$ . . . form$_n$). When the LET form is evaluated, all variables in varlist have their current values saved, and they are each bound to the value NIL. Then the form$_i$ are evaluated, the variables in varlist are rebound to their original values, and the value of form$_n$ is returned as the value of the LET form. A more intricate option is allowed. The variables in the varlist of LET may be initialized to values other than NIL. This allows the effects of SETQ without actually using it. To provide a non-NIL initial value for a variable, include it as the CAR of a list whose CADR is a form whose value is to be the initial value of the variable. To use this feature in APPLY-RULE, we do:

```
(DE APPLY-RULE (S RULE)
   (LET ((LP (MATCH (LHS RULE) S)))
        (COND (LP
               (SUBSTITUTE (RHS RULE) LP))
              (T S)))).
```

This more general LET form is: (LET ((var$_1$ val$_1$) . . . (var$_n$ val$_n$)) form$_1$ . . . form$_m$). It is almost, but not quite, equivalent to

```
(LET (var₁ . . . varₙ)
     (SETQ var₁ val₁ . . . varₙ valₙ)
     form₁ . . . formₘ).
```

The difference is that SETQ assigns the variables in order as they are listed, but LET assigns them in parallel. We will examine this further in the exercises. Franz LISP and MACLISP also have the FSUBR* LET* which is exactly like LET, but assigns the variables in order as SETQ does.

Exercises

1. Does your LISP have functions like LET and LET*?

2. Define MYLET as a macro to act like LET. It should transform

    (LET ((var₁ val₁) . . . (varₙ valₙ))
        form₁ . . . formₘ)

    into

    ((LAMBDA (var₁ . . . varₙ)
            form₁ . . . formₘ)
     val₁ . . . valₙ).

3. Load your MATCHING file, and do Exercise 3.1.10 again. Now re-define APPLY-RULE using the first version of LET (use the one you defined, if your LISP doesn't have it), and test it again. You should notice that now LP's value at the top level is not changed by the call to APPLY-RULE. Now use the second version of LET, and test it again.

4. Make the top-level value of X be (A B C), and the top-level value of Y be (D E F). Evaluate

    (LET (X Y)
        (SETQ X '(G H I) Y (CAR X))
        (LIST X Y)).

    Is the SETQ done in sequence or in parallel? Have the top-level values of X and Y been changed?

5. Now evaluate

    (LET ((X '(G H I)) (Y (CAR X)))
        (LIST X Y)).

    Is the assignment in LET done in sequence or in parallel?

6. If your LISP has LET*, evaluate

    (LET* ((X '(G H I)) (Y (CAR X)))
        (LIST X Y)).

    Is the assignment in LET* done in sequence or in parallel? Have the top-level values of S and Y been changed?

3.4 Iteration, Part 1—PROG

In Section 2.7, we introduced recursion as one "method for repeating a computation over and over until some condition is found." Another such method is *iteration*. Although recursion is more in the "spirit" of LISP than iteration, iterative constructs have been included in LISP for those programmers who prefer them. There are even cases, as we shall see, when iteration is preferable to recursion.

As a good example to begin our discussion of iteration, let's again consider the function REVERSE1 of Section 2.9. REVERSE1 takes one list as its argument, and returns a copy of that list with its top elements reversed. The definition of REVERSE1 is:

    (DE REVERSE1 (L) (REVERSE2 L NIL)).

REVERSE1 actually does nothing by itself, but calls its help function, REVERSE2, a recursive function which takes two lists as arguments and returns the reverse of its first list appended to its second list. The definition of REVERSE2 is:

    (DE REVERSE2 (L1 L2)
       (COND ((NULL L1) L2)
             (T (REVERSE2
                 (CDR L1)
                 (CONS (CAR L1) L2))))).

We could express REVERSE2 in English as:

If L1 is empty, then return L2.
Otherwise,
    return the REVERSE2 of (CDR L1)
                   and (CONS (CAR L1) L2).

This is an appropriate recursive way to think of this operation. An iterative way to think of the operation performed by REVERSE2 would be:

Step 1:   If L1 is empty, then terminate and return L2.
Step 2:   Change L2 to (CONS (CAR L1) L2).
Step 3:   Change L1 to (CDR L1).
Step 4:   Go to Step 1.

The LISP function that provides iteration is PROG. PROG is an FSUBR*, which means that: it is a precompiled function available in LISP; it takes an arbitrary number of arguments; it gets its arguments unevaluated and controls the evaluation of them itself. The format for a use of PROG is:

    (PROG varlist s_1 . . . s_n)

where varlist is a list of variables, as for DE, LAMBDA, or the "simple" form of LET, but referred to as "PROG variables," and each s_i is a literal atom or a form. When a PROG form is evaluated, the following happens:

1.   The current values of the PROG variables are saved.
2.   Each PROG variable is bound to NIL.
3.   Let i be 1.

4. If i is greater than n, restore the PROG variables to their saved values, and return NIL as the value of the PROG form.

5a. If s_i is a literal atom (called a *label*), ignore it.

5b. Else, if s_i is (RETURN s), evaluate the S-expression s, restore the PROG variables to their saved values, and return the value of s as the value of the PROG.

5c. Else, if s_i is (GO s_j) and s_j (unevaluated) is an atom in the PROG form, set i to j, and go to step (5).

5d. Else, evaluate s_i, set i to $i+1$, and go to step (5).

PROG does two things: it establishes a local environment for PROG variables, as LET does; it allows the order of evaluation of a sequence of forms to be controlled by two *control forms*—RETURN and GO. LET does not allow the control forms; it only provides the local environment.

(RETURN s) takes one S-expression, s, as its argument. It causes the PROG it is inside to terminate and return the value of s as its value. Naturally, between the time s is evaluated and the PROG returns, the PROG values are restored to their old values. Using RETURN is the only way to get a PROG to return anything but NIL.

(GO atom) takes one atom, unevaluated, as its argument. This atom must be one that appears as a label in the current PROG. The effect of the GO is to cause the next s_i to be considered by the PROG to be the one after the label. Some LISPs allow the argument of GO to be a form, in which case it is evaluated, and its value must be a label. We will ignore this option.

The control forms need not be top-level arguments of PROG. They can appear within other forms. It is most common for them to appear within CONDs. (Is it obvious why?) In some LISPs, they needn't even be textually within the PROG. They can be called from functions called from within the PROG. In that case (RETURN s) means terminate the (dynamically) innermost PROG, returning the value of s, and (GO atom) means go to the form following the label atom in the (dynamically) innermost PROG. However, since this use of GO is so confusing, some LISPS don't allow it. We will examine these options further in the exercises.

Several points about PROG need stressing:

1. PROG always returns NIL, unless it terminates because RETURN is called. Forgetting this is an extremely common mistake, because one gets used to the normal LISP behavior of a form's returning the value of the last S-expression evaluated within it.

2. Since the only value that can be returned by a PROG is the value of the argument of a RETURN, most forms within a PROG have their values ignored. Therefore, they must be used *solely* for their side-effects. Using PROG removes one from the normal appli-

cative style of LISP programming and places one in the FOR-
TRAN-ALGOL-BASIC imperative style. That is what PROG is
for, but especially while learning LISP, you should guard against
overusing it.

3. One of the most valuable features of PROG is that it provides
    local PROG variables. These may be changed by SETQ within
    the PROG without affecting their values in the outer environment.

4. RETURN and GO are *only* legal dynamically within a PROG, and
    for some LISPs they are only legal textually within a PROG.

5. A PROG form is like any other form in LISP—it may appear
    almost anywhere in other forms, although it is most common as
    the only form in a function definition.

Let's now return to our iterative version of REVERSE2. Using PROG,
we can define it as:

```
(DE REVERSE2 (L1 L2)
   (PROG ()
      STEP1 (COND ((NULL L1) (RETURN L2)))
            (SETQ L2 (CONS (CAR L1) L2))
            (SETQ L1 (CDR L1))
            (GO STEP1))).
```

Note that the COND has only one COND pair, and when L1 is not NIL,
we will have a COND with no pair chosen. Most LISPs allow this in all
situations— if no pair of a COND is chosen, the COND just returns NIL
(the value of the last S-expression evaluated), but all LISPs allow this
within a PROG, since it is comparable to the if-then statement without an
else clause. STEP1 is being used as a label, and this version of REVERSE2
does just what the iterative English version does. However, the original
REVERSE2 was introduced as a help function for only two reasons—we
needed an extra variable to hold the reverse of the initial part of the original
list, and the recursion had to be done on the two-argument help function
rather than on the one-argument main function. This version doesn't use
recursion at all, and we can use the PROG to introduce the auxiliary
variable, so we no longer need a help function.

We will call our final iterative reverse function REVERSE3:

```
(REVERSE3 L) EXPR
   Returns a copy of the list L
   with the top-level elements in reverse order
(DE REVERSE3 (L)
   (PROG (RESULT)
      LOOP (COND ((NULL L) (RETURN RESULT)))
```

```
(SETQ RESULT (CONS (CAR L) RESULT)
      L (CDR L))
(GO LOOP)))
```

The additional changes we made were to use RESULT and LOOP for their mnemonic values, rather than L2 and STEP1, and to use the multi-argument SETQ.

It is normally thought that iterative functions are faster and take less space to run than recursive functions. The reasoning is that since function calls take a relatively long time (e.g., to save, bind, and restore lambda variables), iterative loops are faster than recursive loops. Moreover, since recursion requires saving multiple environments, recursive loops require more space than iterative loops (where they can be used). It doesn't always work out that way, however. Since LISP is basically a recursive language, most modern LISPs perform recursion very efficiently. In some cases, an interpreted LISP recursive function will even be faster than an interpreted iterative version of the same function, although when the functions are compiled, the comparison may switch. Interpreted recursive functions will generally take more space than the interpreted iterative version, but some compilers can automatically change some occurrences of recursion (those cases known as "tail recursion") into iteration. For example, the recursive version of REVERSE2 might be compiled into the same code as the iterative version of REVERSE2. In any case, some recursive functions cannot be expressed iteratively (without simulating recursion), such as the function DEPTH of Section 2.10. The best advice is to let the problem determine your approach. Some problems just "feel" recursive, while others "feel" iterative, but to develop this feel requires extensive practice in both styles.

Exercises

1. Using SETQ, give X, Y, and Z the values 1, 2, and 3, respectively, at the top level of LISP. Then evaluate (PROG (Y) (SETQ X 11) (SETQ Y 12) (SETQ Z (PLUS X Y))). What did this PROG return? What are the top-level values of X, Y, and Z now?

2. Evaluate (PROG (Y) (SETQ X 22) (RETURN (SETQ Y 24)) (SETQ Z (PLUS X Y))). What does this PROG return? What are the top-level values of X, Y, and Z now?

3. Evaluate (PROG (X) (SETQ X 33) (GO LABEL) (SETQ Y 36) LABEL (RETURN (SETQ Z (PLUS X Y)))). What does this PROG return? What are the top-level values of X, Y, and Z now?

4. Can you use a RETURN that is not textually within a PROG? To find out, define the function EXIT-PROG as (DE EXIT-PROG () (RETURN T)), and try evaluating (EXIT-PROG). What happened? Now evaluate (PROG (Y) (SETQ X 44) (SETQ Y 48) (EXIT-PROG) (SETQ Z (PLUS X Y))). What happened? What does this PROG return? What are the top-level values of X, Y, and Z now?

5. Can you use a GO that is not textually within a PROG? To find out, define the function JUMP as (DE JUMP () (GO LABEL)), and try evaluating (JUMP). What happened? Now evaluate (PROG (X) (SETQ X 55) (JUMP) (SETQ Y 60) LABEL (RETURN (SETQ Z (PLUS X Y)))). What happened? What does this PROG return? What are the top-level values of X, Y, and Z now?

6. Define a recursive function, BUILD-LIST, that will return a list of the first 100 integers (either ascending or descending). Make the top-level value of LONGLIST this list.

7. Define REVERSE1 and the recursive version of REVERSE2. Test them on some short lists, and then test them by evaluating (REVERSE1 LONGLIST).

8. Define the iterative REVERSE3. Test it on some short lists, and then test it on LONGLIST.

9. ALISP has a function (RUNTIME form) which prints how long it takes to evaluate the form. Franz LISP does not have such a function, but does have (PTIME), which returns a list of two elements, the first of which is the total running time so far and the second of which is the total time spent garbage collecting so far. Using PTIME, we can define RUNTIME as follows:

```
(DEFMACRO RUNTIME (FORM)
   `((LAMBDA (OT FV NT)
        (DIFF (CAR NT)
              (CADR NT)
              (DIFF (CAR OT) (CADR OT))))
     (PTIME)
     ,FORM
     (PTIME))).
```

Notice that the first thing this macro does is evaluate the three arguments of the lambda expression, so we don't include the arithmetic calculation in the running time of the form. Either find a function in your LISP comparable to RUNTIME or define your own.

10. Compare the running times of (REVERSE1 LONGLIST) and (REVERSE3 LONGLIST). If your LISP has a built-in reverse function, compare its running time also.

11. If necessary, change BUILD-LIST so that it takes one integer, N, as an argument, and returns a list of the first N integers.

12. Write an iterative version of BUILD-LIST. Call it IBUILD-LIST.

13. Compare the running times of BUILD-LIST and IBUILD-LIST when building lists long enough to show a difference.

14. Try to find an N such that (BUILD-LIST N) runs out of space, but (IBUILD-LIST N) doesn't. If you succeed, find the largest N for which you can compare the running times of (BUILD-LIST N) and (IBUILD-LIST N), and do so.

15. Perform the same study for (REVERSE1 (IBUILD-LIST N)) vs. (REVERSE3 (IBUILD-LIST N)).

3.5 READ and PRINT

Let's consider what our conception of a LISP program is at this point. A LISP program is a main function and a collection of auxiliary and help functions. To use a LISP program, a user must get into LISP, input or load the functions, and evaluate a call to the main function, giving it the appropriate data as arguments. The main function will then return the output as the value of the call. This is precisely the attitude of applicative programming—a program is a function for transforming input into output.

Many programs that are actually written, however, have a different flavor. The typical interactive program prints information out to the user, accepts input data typed by the user, and prints output data to the user. Some of the information typed to the user is in the form of *prompts*, or requests for information, sometimes with directions on what information is desired and how it is to be typed. Notice that LISP, itself, acts like such an interactive program. In fact, LISP *is* such an interactive program. In this section, we will see how to simulate LISP. Notice also that these typical programs we are discussing have an iterative, imperative style. That is why I waited until now to discuss them.

If we are to write one of these typical programs, we need two abilities—the ability to output information to the user and the ability to input data from the user. Most LISPs have many functions to do these jobs in various ways, but the two most important of them are invariably called PRINT and READ, respectively.

In the text of this section, I will make some simplifying assumptions about precisely how PRINT and READ work, but different dialects of

LISP, and LISPs on different computing systems, may work slightly differently. We will examine those differences in the exercises.

CPRINT S) is a SUBR of one argument. It is used for its side-effect, which is to print the value of its argument on the terminal. Of course, PRINT is a LISP function, which means that CPRINT S) also has a value. In some LISPs, like Franz LISP, PRINT always returns NIL. In some LISPs, like MACLISP, PRINT always returns T. In others, like INTERLISP and ALISP, PRINT returns the value of its argument (as well as printing it). A common mistake is forgetting that PRINT takes only one argument. We will see how to overcome this limitation.

READ is a SUBR of *no* arguments. It is used for its value, which is *the next S-expression in the input buffer.* CREAD) also has a side-effect, which is to *consume* that S-expression, so that the next CREAD) doesn't read it again. On some systems, CREAD) also causes a prompt character to be issued.

Notice that I said that READ reads an S-expression. Whether the S-expression is an atom or a list, and no matter over how many lines it extends, READ always reads and returns an entire S-expression. By "the next S-expression in the input buffer," I mean the next S-expression the user has typed or will type. (On some systems, the user can type ahead—even before the READ has been executed—on others, the user must wait for a prompt.)

We can now write our LISP simulator. Remember, top-level LISP cycles through the operations: read an S-expression; evaluate it; print the value. So let's define a LISP simulator. Call it LISP.

CDE LISP () (PRINT (EVAL (READ))) (LISP))

It's that simple! But let's examine it. PRINT is a SUBR, so it gets its argument evaluated. Its argument is a call to EVAL. EVAL is also a SUBR, so it gets its argument evaluated. Its argument is a call to READ. READ has no argument. It reads the next S-expression in the input buffer and returns it (as typed—not evaluated). EVAL then gets what was typed, evaluates it, and returns its value. Then, PRINT prints that value to the terminal. From the user's point of view, the user has typed in an S-expression, and LISP has typed out its value. Finally, the second form in the body of LISP is evaluated. This is a recursive call to LISP itself, so the cycle continues. The only way out is to make an error, or press the interrupt key. That's one reason this is only a simulator.

One problem with this definition of LISP is that it is recursive. As you found out in the last section, if a recursive function calls itself enough times, it may eventually run out of space. It just doesn't make sense that the longer you interact with top-level LISP, the more space you take up and the less you have available for useful work. As I said above, an interactive program is essentially an iterative one, and the LISP READ-

EVAL-PRINT loop should also be an iterative loop. In fact, every interactive program is essentially a READ-EVAL-PRINT iterative loop. This is precisely what I had in mind at the beginning of Section 3.4, when I said, "There are even cases, as we shall see, when iteration is preferable to recursion." I will leave the iterative LISP simulator for you to write as an exercise.

In our LISP simulator, the fact that PRINT takes only one argument didn't bother us, but what if we want to print a long message? For example, we may want to print "Enter a sentence." Notice that (PRINT ENTER A SENTENCE) is incorrect since it gives PRINT three arguments. (It is also incorrect because PRINT evaluates its argument.) There are three solutions:

1) we may enclose our message in a list—
   (PRINT '(ENTER A SENTENCE));
2) we may use the escape character to turn our message into a long atom—(PRINT 'ENTER\ A\ SENTENCE);
3) we may use a string (see Exercise 1.3.10)—
   (PRINT "ENTER A SENTENCE").

The best solution is to use a string (if your LISP has strings)—that's just what strings are for.

What if, however, you want to print a message that mixes a canned message with a computed message. For example, after issuing the ENTER A SENTENCE prompt, we might want to read the sentence and echo out "I heard you say <sentence>", where the actual typed sentence appears instead of "<sentence>"? Let's assume the sentence is bound to the atom SENTENCE. There are two possibilities:

1) we can print a list—
(PRINT (LIST 'I 'HEARD 'YOU 'SAY SENTENCE)),
   or (PRINT (APPEND '(I HEARD YOU SAY)
                     (LIST SENTENCE))),
   or (PRINT `(I HEARD YOU SAY ,SENTENCE));
2) we can write our own print function. Let's do the latter.

Our problem is to write a function that takes an arbitrary number of arguments. Let's make it so that it prints each argument unevaluated, but if one argument is the atom =, instead of printing it and the next argument, it prints the *value* of the next argument.

      (PRINTF* S1 . . . SN) MACRO
               Prints each Si unevaluated,
                    unless it is "=" or is preceded by "=".
               For each pair of arguments, "= S",
                    the value of S is printed

```
(DM PRINTF* (MESSAGE)
   `(MAPC 'PRINT
          (UNQUOTE ,@(CDR MESSAGE)))).
```

MAPC is the name most LISPs give to the mapping function that is just like APPLY-TO-EACH, but which is used for the side-effect achieved by the application of the function to each member of the list, rather than for the list of values. UNQUOTE is the function you wrote for Exercise 2.12.20.

With PRINTF* (and its help function) defined, we may execute (PRINTF* I HEARD YOU SAY = SENTENCE).

Our only problem now is how to read the user's sentence. Since (READ) reads one S-expression, but a sentence is a sequence of words, there is a minor problem. Again, there are two solutions. We could ask the user to type the sentence enclosed in a set of parentheses. This will be read as a single list. Otherwise, we could ask the user to terminate the sentence with some termination symbol. Assuming the function (TERMINATOR SYMB) returns T if SYMB is a terminator we have chosen, and NIL otherwise, the function READASENTENCE could be defined as follows:

> (READASENTENCE) EXPR
>> Reads a sequence of S-expressions until a terminator
>> is encountered.
>> Returns a list of the expressions without the
>> terminator.

```
(DE READASENTENCE ()
   (READASENTENCE1 (READ)))

(DE READASENTENCE1 (WORD)
   (COND ((TERMINATOR WORD) NIL)
         (T (CONS WORD (READASENTENCE)))))
```

Exercises

1. Evaluate (PRINT 'FOO). Notice that LISP has printed two atoms on your terminal: the atom FOO, which you had it print with your call to PRINT, and the value of the S-expression (PRINT 'FOO), since LISP always prints the value of the S-expression you type to it. Some LISPs will print the two atoms on two separate lines, some will print them on the same line separated by a blank, and some will print them on the same line not separated by a blank.

2. What does your LISP return as the value of a call to PRINT: NIL, T, the value of the argument to PRINT, or something else? Write the answer here:

_____.

3. Notice that when you evaluated (PRINT 'FOO), "FOO" was printed on a lower line. That is because you typed a carriage return after typing (PRINT 'FOO). However, if "FOO" and the value of the PRINT were printed on separate lines, that is because your LISP types a carriage return after each PRINT. Does your LISP end each PRINT with a carriage return or not? Write the answer here: _____.

4. If your LISP does not end each PRINT with a carriage return, it might or might not end each PRINT with a blank. Which does it do? Write the answer here: _____.

5. Does your LISP precede each PRINT with a carriage return? To find out, evaluate (PROGN (PRINT 'FOO) (PRINT 'BAR)), and see what appears between the "FOO" and the "BAR". Remember to differentiate what happened after "FOO" was printed from what happened before the "BAR" was printed. Write the answer here:

_____

6. Some LISPs have a function of no arguments whose side-effect is to print a carriage return. Franz LISP and ALISP call it (TERPRI). Does your LISP have such a function? If so, write its name here:

_____

What does it return? Experiment with it.

7. Try evaluating (PRINT ENTER A SENTENCE). Do you get an error message?

8. Evaluate (PRINT '(ENTER A SENTENCE)). Notice how the output looks.

9. Evaluate (PRINT 'ENTER\ A\ SENTENCE). Remember, if "\" is not your escape character, replace it with yours. You may get the escape characters in your printed line, or you might get "escape brackets" around the phrase. For example, Franz LISP prints "❙ENTER A SENTENCE❙". If either of these two things happens to you, see if your LISP has a print function which doesn't print the escape characters. Franz LISP calls it PATOM.

10. Evaluate (PRINT "ENTER A SENTENCE"). Were the quote marks printed? If so, see if your LISP has a way of printing a string without the quote marks.

11. Can you print a blank? Try (PRINT '\ ). If an escape character is printed, see Exercise 9 above.

12. Does your LISP have MAPC, or a function like it? If not, define your own MAPC.

13. Evaluate (MAPC 'PRINT '(ENTER A SENTENCE)). If you do not get a blank between the words, define the function (PRINB

ATM) to print ATM, and then print a blank. Now try (MAPC 'PRINB '(ENTER A SENTENCE)).

14. Redefine UNQUOTE from Exercise 2.12.20. Use macros if you have them.

15. Define PRINTF*. Give SENTENCE the top-level value of HELLO, and try evaluating (PRINTF* I HEARD YOU SAY = SENTENCE). Edit the definition as necessary so that the message appears on one line with words separated by blanks.

16. Edit your PRINTF* so that if one of the argument forms is the atom <> a carriage return is done at that point in the message. Now, (PRINTF* I HEARD YOU SAY <> SENTENCE <>) should print its value on a different line from its message. (Hint: Instead of mapping PRINT, map your own printing function that recognizes <>.)

17. Give SENTENCE the top-level value (THE MOON IN JUNE MAKES ME SPOON), and evaluate (PRINTF* I HEARD YOU SAY = SENTENCE <>). The trouble is that sometimes we want to print the value of an S-expression with its enclosing parentheses and sometimes we don't. Review Exercise 2.16.7, and revise your UNQUOTE to solve this problem.

18. Instead of including a sequence of constant atoms as the arguments of PRINTF*, it is more efficient to make them into one string, e.g., (PRINTF* "I HEARD YOU SAY" = SENTENCE <>). Edit your PRINTF*, if necessary, so that strings are printed without the quote marks.

19. Type (READ)FOO on one line. Is "FOO" read and returned?

20. Type (READ) on one line and FOO on the next. Do you have to wait for a prompt?

21. Try giving your (READ) an S-expression that extends over more than one line. Do you have to wait for a prompt on each line?

22. Can you read more than one S-expression on one line? To find out, evaluate (PROGN (PRINT (READ)) (PRINT (READ))).

23. Define and test the LISP simulator as shown in the text. Is there any difference between the READ you are using and the one top-level LISP uses? To find out, you might do the exercises of Sections 1.2, 1.3, and 1.4 under the control of your LISP.

24. Redefine the LISP simulator as an iterative function. What happens if you give your simulator the form (RETURN)? (See Exercise 3.4.4.)

25. The top-level LISP we have been discussing is sometimes called EVAL

LISP, because of its READ-EVAL-PRINT loop. There are some LISPs, called EVALQUOTE LISPs, that work differently at the top level. They read two S-expressions at a time. The first must be the name of a function or a lambda expression. The second must be a list of the actual arguments being passed to the function. The value of the first expression applied to the second is then printed. For example, one might type the following lines to an EVALQUOTE LISP:

```
CAR ((A B C))
CONS (A (B C))
```

Edit your LISP simulator so that it is an EVALQUOTE LISP simulator.

26. Choose one or more sentence termination symbols (atoms), and define (TERMINATOR SYMB) so that it returns T if SYMB is a terminator and NIL otherwise.

27. Define and test READASENTENCE.

28. Define an iterative READ-EVAL-PRINT loop that prompts the user for a sentence, reads it, and then echoes it preceded by "I HEARD YOU SAY".

29. Load your MATCHING file. Define an iterative READ-EVAL-PRINT loop that reads a sentence, and prints the result of transforming it with APPLY-RULES. Use rules like ((X THINKS I AM Y) (DO YOU THINK YOU ARE Y)) and ((I THINK I AM X) (HOW LONG HAVE YOU BEEN X)). You have now written a miniature version of the famous ELIZA program, written by Joseph Weizenbaum in the 1960s.

30. Retrieve the functions from your file COMPUTE. Define a READ-EVAL-PRINT loop that reads an arithmetic expression in normal infix notation, and prints its value. Be sure to save it in COMPUTE. Under the control of this READ-EVAL-PRINT loop, redo Exercises 1.5.8 and 1.6.9. You have now written an interactive desk calculator.

3.6 Iteration, Part 2

PROG was introduced into LISP before the structured programming movement, which, among other things, stressed structured loops, such as WHILE and UNTIL, and programming without using GO. Pure LISP, of course, already satisfied all the criteria of structured programming, but the non-pure part of LISP was introduced for those who liked the non-applicative style, and it relied heavily on GO. Therefore, over the years, people introduced structured loops into their local versions of LISP by defining them as macros. Now that some of these versions of LISP have developed into major dialects, we have the situation that most modern LISPs have one or more structured loop constructs, but no one structured loop construct is universal. In this section, I will discuss one structured loop that is fairly widespread (at least four LISPs use it); one structured loop that is not widespread, but is quite clear; and how you might start to define your own structured loop.

Franz LISP, MACLISP, Zetalisp, and Common Lisp all use a structured loop function called DO. The format of DO is:

(DO varspeclist test form$_1$ . . . form$_n$).

The form$_i$ constitute the body of the loop. They are evaluated in order each time through the loop. However, the RETURN and GO control forms of PROG are allowed in a DO body, and they can the change the order of evaluation.

Varspeclist is a list of specifications of local variables. Each variable is specified in one of three ways. The first two are exactly as in LET: an atomic variable is initially bound to NIL; a (var val) pair specifies that the initial value of var is to be the value of val. The third specification format is a triple, (var val loopval), specifying that the initial value of var is to be the value of val, and that every time through the loop, the value of val is to be changed to the value of loopval. As in LET, rather than LET*, the initial values are assigned to the variables in parallel. One varspeclist may contain a mixture of these three formats, but to help you visualize them, here they are separated:

```
(DO           (... var ...)           test forms)
(DO          (... (var val) ...)      test forms)
(DO (... (var val loopval) ...) test forms)
```

Test has three possible formats. If test is (), the forms are just evaluated once, no looping is done, and the DO returns NIL. This is essentially just a PROG with the variable initialization feature of LET. If the test is (p), where p is any S-expression, then just before the loop body is entered each time, p is evaluated. If p evaluates to NIL, the loop body is evaluated at least one more time. If p evaluates to anything other than NIL (i.e., to True), the DO returns with the value of NIL. If the test is (p e$_1$ . . . e$_m$), where p and the e$_i$ are any S-expressions, then just before the loop body is entered each time, p is evaluated. If p evaluates to NIL, the loop body is evaluated at least one more time. If p evaluates to anything other than NIL (i.e., to True), the e$_i$ are evaluated in order and the DO returns with the value of e$_m$. Table 3.2

summarizes this:

Table 3.2

`CDO varspeclist ()` `    form₁ . . . formₙ)`	Loop once; Return NIL
`CDO varspeclist (p)` `    form₁ . . . formₙ)`	Until p loop; Return NIL

`CDO varspeclist`
`    (p e₁ . . . eₘ)`
`    form₁ . . . formₙ)`
	Until p loop; Return val of eₘ

As examples, we shall define MEMBER and REVERSE using DO:

```
(MEMBER A L) EXPR
    MEMBER returns True
    if the atom A is a member of the list L,
    NIL otherwise.
(DE MEMBER (A L)
   (DO ( (LL L (CDR LL)) )
       ( (OR (NULL LL) (EQ (CAR LL) A))
         LL ) ))
```

```
(REVERSE L) EXPR
    Returns the reverse of the list L.
(DE REVERSE (L)
   (DO ( (LL L (CDR LL))
         (RL NIL (CONS (CAR LL) RL)) )
       ( (NULL LL) RL ) ))
```

Both of these are interesting because they have no bodies—all the work is done in the var specl ists. Notice that there are two reasons for terminating MEMBER—LL is null or the CAR of LL is A—and that in both cases LL is the right answer. Also notice that this definition of REVERSE depends on the loopvals being assigned to the local variables in parallel.

ALISP has a particularly clear and simple structured loop construct, that is, nevertheless, quite flexible. Its one drawback when compared with DO is that it requires more explicit uses of SETQ. However, you might view this as favorable clarity. This loop is called REPEAT, and its format is:

```
(REPEAT varlist s₁ . . . sₙ).
```

Varlist is a list of local variables as in PROG. The sᵢ are also as in

PROG, except there are three special control labels. The atom BEGIN may appear at most once. If it does appear, all s_i before BEGIN are for initialization only; the loop body begins with the S-expression after BEGIN. If it does not appear, all S-expressions are part of the loop body. The atom WHILE may appear anywhere in the loop body except as the last S-expression, and any number of times. When WHILE is reached in the evaluation of the S-expressions, the next one is evaluated, and if it evaluates to NIL, the REPEAT is immediately exited, returning the value of NIL. If that S-expression evaluates to a non-NULL value, the loop continues. The atom UNTIL may appear anywhere in the loop body except as the last S-expression, and any number of times. When UNTIL is reached in the evaluation of the S-expressions, the next one is evaluated, and if it evaluates to a non-NULL value, the REPEAT is immediately exited, returning that value. If the S-expression evaluates to NIL, the loop continues. After s_n is evaluated, the loop continues with the first S-expression in the loop body. As is usual in LISP, the value returned by REPEAT is always the value of the last S-expression evaluated within its control.

The paradigm use of REPEAT is to define MEMBER:

```
(DE MEMBER (A L)
   (REPEAT ()
     WHILE L
     UNTIL (EQ (CAR L) A)
        (SETQ L (CDR L)))).
```

REVERSE, however, does not benefit from the special keywords of REPEAT:

```
(DE REVERSE (L)
   (REPEAT (RL)
           (COND ((NULL L) (RETURN RL)))
           (SETQ RL (CONS (CAR L) RL)
           L (CDR L)))).
```

Although the combination of LET and REPEAT looks nice:

```
(DE REVERSE (L)
   (LET (RL)
        (REPEAT ()
          WHILE L
                (SETQ RL (CONS (CAR L) RL)
                      L (CDR L)))
        RL))
```

Some other dialects of LISP have structured loops similar to REPEAT in that they are controlled by special atoms and one or more forms that appear after them.

Finally, let's look at a simple way to define our own structured loops, making use only of PROG and macros. Our structured loop will be called LOOP, and will have the format:

```
(LOOP varlist form₁ . . . formₙ)
```

where varlist will be as in LET, and the formᵢ will form the body of the loop, and be as in PROG. In addition, BEGIN will function as in REPEAT; (LOOPNEXT) will send evaluation from wherever it is to the beginning of the loop body; (WHILE p e₁ . . . eₙ) will evaluate p, and if it is non-NULL, remain in the loop, but if it is NIL, will evaluate the eᵢ in order and terminate the loop returning the value of eₙ, or the value of p if there are no eᵢ; (UNTIL p e₁ . . . eₙ) will evaluate p, and if it is NIL, remain in the loop, but if it is non-NULL, will evaluate the eᵢ in order and terminate the loop returning the value of eₙ, or the value of p if there are no eᵢ. Naturally, (RETURN form) will cause the loop to be terminated, returning the value of form. The required function definitions for our LOOP are:

```
(DM LOOP (LOOP-VARLIST-FORMS)
  '(LET
    ,(CADR LOOP-VARLIST-FORMS)
    (PROG ()
      ,@(COND
          ((MEMBER 'BEGIN
                   LOOP-VARLIST-FORMS)
           (APPEND
            (CDDR LOOP-VARLIST-FORMS)
            '((GO BEGIN))))
          (T (CONS
              'BEGIN
              (APPEND
               (CDDR LOOP-VARLIST-FORMS)
               '((GO BEGIN)))))))))

(DM LOOPNEXT () '(GO BEGIN))

(DM WHILE (FVAL)
  '(LET ((P ,(CADR FVAL)))
     (COND ((NULL P)
            (RETURN
             (PROGN P
                    ,@(CDDR FVAL)))))))
```

```
(DM UNTIL (FVAL)
   '(LET ((P ,(CADR FVAL)))
        (COND (P
                (RETURN
                  (PROGN P
                          ,@(CDDR FVAL)))))))).
```

Using LOOP, MEMBER and REVERSE are:

```
(DE MEMBER (A L)
   (LOOP ()
        (WHILE L)
        (UNTIL (EQ (CAR L) A))
        (SETQ L (CDR L))))
```

```
(DE REVERSE (L)
   (LOOP (RL)
        (UNTIL (NULL L) RL)
        (SETQ RL (CONS (CAR L) RL)
              L (CDR L))))
```

(Note: This MEMBER returns NIL or T, rather than NIL or a tail of L.)

Several dialects of LISP have structured loops like our LOOP, in that their control forms look like function calls. However, be careful when reading your manual. Some of them look like our LOOP, but wherever you put the control forms in the loop body, they will move them either to the beginning or to the end. Our LOOP, like REPEAT, allows WHILEs and UNTILs scattered among the other forms.

Exercises

1. Does your LISP have a structured loop? If so, study it carefully to see if it is like any we have discussed in this section.

2. If your structured loop has local variables, evaluate your version of: (DO (X Y) () (PRINT X) (PRINT Y)) to see what the variables of a simple varlist are initialized to.

3. If your structured loop supports a varspeclist like LET's, first set the top-level value of X to '(A B C), then evaluate your version of: (DO ((X '(X Y Z)) (Y (CAR X))) () (PRINT X) (PRINT Y)) to see if the initialization works like LET or like LET*.

4. If your structured loop has a test form like DO's, try evaluating

```
(DO ((X '(A S D F G H)))
    ()
    (PRINT X) (TERPRI)
    (SETQ X (CDR X)))
```

to see if the ( ) format evaluates the body only once, and to see what is returned.

5. If your structured loop has a test form like DO's, try evaluating

```
(DO ((X '(A S D F G H) (CDR X)))
    ((EQ (CAR X) 'F))
    (PRINT X) (TERPRI))
```

to see if the (p) format always returns NIL.

6. Use your structured loop to define MYMEMBER. Does (MYMEMBER 'A '(S A D)) return T, or (A D)?

7. Use your structured loop to define MYREVERSE.

8. Define LOOP as in this section. The MEMBER used in the definition of LOOP should be your LISP's MEMBER.

9. Define MYMEMBER and MYREVERSE using the LOOP you just defined.

10. Define a structured loop with the format

```
(FOR var FROM initval
         TO finalval
         BY stepval
    form₁ . . . formₙ).
```

The $form_i$ should constitute the loop body. Var should be a local variable. Initval, finalval, and stepval should evaluate to numbers. Var should be initialized to the value of initval. Each time before evaluating the body, val should be compared to finalval. If finalval is greater than initval, the loop should be executed only if the value of val is not yet greater than finalval. If finalval is smaller than initval, the loop should be executed only if the value of val is not yet smaller than finalval. At the end of the loop, val should be incremented by the value of stepval. Of course, the sign of stepval should be such that var is brought closer to finalval at each loop. You decide what your FOR should return.

3.7 Destructive List Manipulation

Throughout this book, so far, I have been warning you against using any destructive list manipulation functions. The time has come to discuss them, but the warning still holds—do not use these functions unless you really understand what you are doing. A mistake can lead to strange errors that are extremely difficult to find.

First, we have to understand how LISP represents lists. Whenever LISP evaluates a call to CONS, it gets some computer memory from a place called the "available space list," or simply, "free space." This memory is configured as a *cons cell*. A cons cell may be thought of as a *record* with two *fields*. The two fields are called the CAR and the CDR. Each field contains a *pointer* to the representation of an S-expression. If that S-expression is a list, the pointer will point to another cons cell which represents that list.

We can draw cons cells in a graphical style that has become known as *box notation*. A cons cell looks like a rectangle, divided in two halves. The left half is the CAR, and the right half is the CDR. If a field holds a pointer to an atom, we will just show that atom's pname in its field. So, the picture of the value of (CONS 'CAR 'CDR) is:

This is the box notation for the dotted pair (CAR . CDR).

If a CDR field contains a pointer to NIL, we will just show a diagonal line through that field. So, the box notation for (CONS 'A NIL), which is the dotted pair (A . NIL), and also the list (A), is:

However, we will show the box notation of (CONS NIL NIL), which is the dotted pair (NIL . NIL), and the list (NIL), as:

If a field contains a pointer to another cons cell, we will show it as an arrow from the field to the cell. So, the box notation for the list (A B C) is:

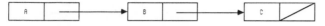

Remember, in dotted pair notation, this is (A . (B . (C . NIL))).

A CAR might also contain a pointer to a cons cell. The box notation for the list (A (B C) D) is:

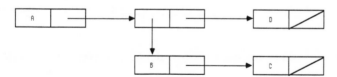

Remember that when you define a function, a lambda form is stored either as the value of the function name or in a special place accessible from the function name by an access function such as GETD. (See Section 2.2.) A lambda form is also a list. For example, we might want to define the function ⟨HOPEFUL L⟩, which simply appends ⟨I HOPE⟩ to its argument list. After doing

```
(DE HOPEFUL (L)
        (APPEND L '(I HOPE)))
```

the value of ⟨GETD 'HOPEFUL⟩ is the lambda form

```
(LAMBDA (L)
                (APPEND L '(I HOPE)))
```

In box notation, this lambda form is:

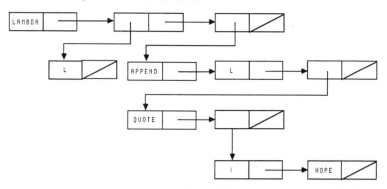

When you give an atom a value via SETQ, or by binding it when a lambda form is applied, or when a PROG, LET, DO, etc., is entered, what is stored in the atom's *value cell* is a pointer to the S-expression that the atom was bound to. We can picture the result of ⟨SETQ X '⟨A B C⟩⟩ as:

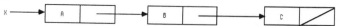

If we now do ⟨SETQ Y ⟨CDR X⟩⟩, a copy of the actual pointer in the CDR field of the cons cell that X points to is placed in the value cell of Y, giving:

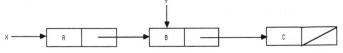

Earlier, I said that EQ tests for identity, so two lists are seldom EQ,

even if they are EQUAL. Actually, EQ compares pointers, and returns T
if the pointers are equal. In the above case, (EQ Y (CDR X)) would
return T because Y and the CDR field of X point to the same cons cell.
However, (EQ Y '(B C)) would evaluate to NIL, because two new
cons cells would be used to construct the list (B C) in that case.

If this view of LISP is now understood, we are ready to talk about
destructive list manipulation. The two basic destructive list manipulation
functions are (RPLACA S1 S2) and (RPLACD S1 S2). They stand
for RePLACe CAr, and RePLACe CDr, respectively, and are SUBRs,
evaluating both their arguments. In the case of both these functions, the
value of the first argument must be a cons cell. (RPLACA S1 S2)
changes the CAR field of S1 so that it points to S2. (RPLACD S1
S2) *changes* the CDR field of S1 so that it points to S2. Both return
the newly changed cons cell. Let's look at the above diagram after doing
(RPLACA Y 'D):

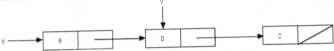

The cons cell Y points to is now (D C). Therefore, the value of Y is
now (D C). Y seems to have a new value, although it really doesn't. Y
still points to the same cons cell it pointed to before; it is the contents of
that cons cell that has changed. Moreover, X has also been changed! It is
now (A D C), even though the form (RPLACA Y 'D) didn't mention X. That is why destructive list manipulation is so dangerous. By changing one thing, you can change something else that apparently has nothing
to do with it.

If we now did (RPLACD Y '(E F)), the picture would change to:

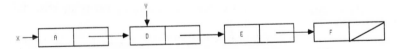

and X would have the value (A D E F).

Earlier we looked at APPEND and noted that APPEND makes a copy
of its first argument, but reuses its second argument. If X were (A B),
Y were (C D), and we did (SETQ Z (APPEND X Y)), we would
get the following situation:

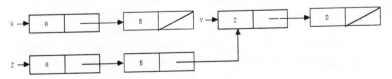

(EQ X Z) would be NIL, but (EQ Y (CDDR Z)) would be T, and if we now did (RPLACA Y 'E), Z would change to (A B E D).

There is also a destructive version of APPEND, which most LISPs call NCONC. (NCONC L1 L2) CDRs down L1 until it finds the last cons cell, then does a RPLACD on that cell, changing its CDR to point to L2. Again, if X were (A B), and Y were (C D), and we did (SETQ Z (NCONC X Y)), we would get:

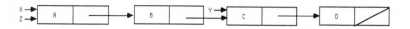

X and Z would now be EQ, as well as EQUAL.

What if X were (A B), and we did (NCONC X X)? The picture would be:

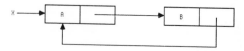

The second cons cell of X would have a CDR pointing to the first cons cell of X. This is an infinite list: (A B A B A B . . .). The only way to get infinite lists in LISP is with destructive list manipulation.

We could get another kind of infinite list by starting with X as (A B), and doing (RPLACA (CDR X) X). We would then get:

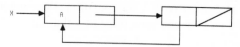

Here X is a sublist of itself: (A (A (A ...))).

The possibility of accidentally making an infinite list is another danger of destructive list manipulation.

Destructive list manipulation is not all bad. There are some good uses for it—if you are careful. One benefit of it is the saving of time and space. If you never use destructive list manipulation, you will use a lot of new cons cells from free space. Most of these will be used for only a short time and then be discarded. We call such cons cells *garbage*. Eventually, all of free space will have been used. Then, if we want some more, a special LISP function called the *garbage collector* will automatically be executed, and will look through the computer memory we are using to find and collect the garbage, and reconstitute free space. The garbage collector takes a while to operate, and slows down our program. Nevertheless, automatic garbage collection is one of the major features of LISP. Other languages make the programmers keep track of their own garbage, and recycle it themselves. Use of destructive list manipulation, in appropriate places, will generate less garbage and require the garbage collector less often. However, when in doubt, don't use it!

One useful destructive list manipulation function is a mapping function sometimes called MAPCAN and sometimes called MAPCONC. It is like MAPCAR (APPLY-TO-EACH), but NCONCs all the results together before returning. Notice that if we NCONC the elements of the list ((A B) (C) () (D E)) we get (A B C D E). In particular, empty lists disappear. We can use this for writing a "filter" function that takes a predicate and a list and returns a list containing only those elements of the original list for which the predicate is True:

```
(DE FILTER (P L)
   (MAPCAN
      '(LAMBDA (E)
               (COND ((FUNCALL P E) (LIST E))
                     (T NIL)))
      L)).
```

FUNCALL is like APPLY, but takes each argument of the function it is applying as a separate argument of its own, instead of taking them all in a list. (FUNCALL 'CONS 'A '(B)) does just what (APPLY 'CONS '(A (B))) does. Some LISPs use APPLY* instead of FUNCALL.

One interesting use of FILTER is the quicksort function (QSORT L). This works by dividing its argument list L into three lists: those elements less than its CAR, those EQ to its CAR, those greater than its CAR. It then recursively sorts the first and third lists and NCONCs the three together. (In some LISPs, NCONC is a SUBR*, taking an arbitrary number of lists.) This version of quicksort traverses the list more times than the traditional version, but it is also much clearer.

```
(DEF QSORT
   (LAMBDA (L)
      (COND
         ((NULL L) NIL)
         ((NULL (CDR L)) L)
         (T (NCONC
              (QSORT
                (FILTER
                  '(LAMBDA (N)
                           (LESSP N (CAR L)))
                  L))
              (FILTER
                '(LAMBDA (N)
                         (EQ N (CAR L)))
                L)
```

```
(QSORT
    (FILTER
        '(LAMBDA (N)
                (GREATERP N (CAR L)))
        L)))))))
```

Destructive list manipulation is also useful when you are maintaining some large data structure in a global variable and want to change parts of it without copying large parts of it unneccessarily. One common example of this is LISP structure editors. The definition of a function is stored in a globally accessible structure. If you use a LISP-based structure editor, it works by destructive list manipulation of the function definition.

Exercises

1. Set X to (A B C) and Y to (CDR X). What is the value of (EQ Y (CDR X))? What is the value of (EQ Y '(B C))?

2. Do (RPLACA Y 'D). What is the value of Y now? What is the value of X?

3. Do (RPLACD Y '(E F)). What is the value of Y now? What is the value of X?

4. Set X to (A B), Y to (C D), and Z to (APPEND X Y). What is the value of X now? What is the value of (EQ Y (CDDR Z))?

5. Set X to (A B), Y to (C D), and Z to (NCONC X Y). What is the value of X now? What is the value of (EQ Y (CDDR Z))? What is the value of (EQ X Z)?

6. Can your LISP's NCONC take an arbitrary number of arguments, or only two?

7. Make sure you remember your LISP's interrupt key. Then set X to (A B). Then do (NCONC X X).

8. Set X back to (A B). Then do (RPLACA (CDR X) X).

9. Define HOPEFUL as in this section. Pretty-print the definition, so you remember it.

10. Make H point to the lambda form defining HOPEFUL by doing your LISP's version of (SETQ H (GETD 'HOPEFUL)). Now change H so that it points to the instance of the list (I HOPE) in the definition. You can do this by an appropriate sequence of (SETQ H (CAR H)) and (SETQ H (CDR H)), while looking at the box notation version of the lambda form.

11. Define (EMPHATIC L) to NCONC the list (VERY MUCH) onto the end of its argument list.

12. Set the top-level value of S to (I AM A GOOD LISPER), and then do (SETQ SS (EMPHATIC (HOPEFUL S))). Pretty-print your definition of HOPEFUL again. What happened? What is the value of H now? This is another danger of destructive list manipulation—function definitions can be changed.

13. Now evaluate (EMPHATIC (HOPEFUL '(I KNOW WHAT I AM DOING))). Make sure you know what happened and why.

14. LISPs generally allow you to force a garbage collection whenever you want. You may want to do this during interaction with the user, when the time the garbage collector takes won't be noticed, and start a moderately long calculation with as much free space as possible. In most LISPs you do this by evaluating the function of no arguments (GC), although in INTERLISP, it is (RECLAIM 'LISTP). How do you do it in your LISP? Write it here:

_____ .

15. In many LISPs, you can get the garbage collector to print something to the terminal when it finishes, so you know it has been called. In Franz LISP, you turn on this reporting by doing (SETQ $GCPRINT T). In UCI LISP and INTERLISP, you do (GCGAG T). What do you do in your LISP? Write it here: _____ .
Do it. Then call the garbage collector to make sure the reporting works.

16. Define the following infinitely looping function, whose sole purpose is to consume free space and generate garbage as quickly as possible. Use whatever iterative construct is most convenient. I will use the LOOP we wrote in SECTION 3.6.

```
(DE EAT ()
    (LOOP ( (N 0) (L NIL) )
          (SETQ N (ADD1 N)
                L (APPEND L (LIST N)))
          (PRINT N)
          (TERPRI)))
```

Call the garbage collector once more, then evaluate (EAT), keeping your finger on the interrupt key. Interrupt as soon as the garbage collector is called. How far did the loop get? Now edit EAT, changing APPEND to NCONC, and try this again. Did you get further?

17. What is your LISP's version of FUNCALL? Write its name here:

_____ .

18. Define F I L T E R as in this section, and test it. A good test is (F I L T E R
    ' N U M B E R P ' (A 1 S 2 D)).

19. Define Q S O R T as in this section, and test it. Make sure that one of
    your tests is with a list with some number appearing more than once.

20. Define H O P E F U L again as given in this section. Set H to the lambda
    form defining H O P E F U L by doing your LISP's version of (S E T Q H
    (G E T D ' H O P E F U L)).

21. Set HL to the list (Q U O T E (I H O P E)) occurring within the S-
    expression H, by doing what you did in Exercise 10 above.

22. Using destructive list manipulation, change HL to (L I S T ' I
    ' H O P E). The change should be reflected in the value of H, and in
    the pretty-printed version of H O P E F U L. You have just simulated a
    structure editor.

23. If you have a structure editor, define E M P H A T I C as first given in
    this section, and set E to the lambda form defining it. Now using your
    structure editor, change (Q U O T E (V E R Y M U C H)) to (L I S T
    ' V E R Y ' M U C H). What is the value of E now?

24. If you don't have a structure editor, just redefine E M P H A T I C re-
    placing (N C O N C L ' (V E R Y M U C H)) by (N C O N C L (L I S T
    ' V E R Y ' M U C H)).

25. Do Exercises 12 and 13 again. You now know the safe way to define
    functions like H O P E F U L and E M P H A T I C.

3.8 Property Lists

We have seen several pieces of information associated with literal atoms.
First, a literal atom can have a value, stored in a place called the *value
cell* of the atom. Whenever LISP enters an environment where the atom
is a local variable (i.e., a lambda, PROG, LET, etc., variable), the value
in the value cell is saved somewhere else, and replaced by another value.
When the environment is left, the saved value is replaced in the value cell,
and what had been there is discarded.

A literal atom can also have a function definition associated with it. In
a few LISPs (for example, ALISP), the function definition is also put in
the value cell. This means that an atom cannot simultaneously be a local
variable and the name of a function, because while it has some other value
its function definition is unavailable. However, it also means that we can
have new definitions temporarily replace old ones within an environment.
This is sometimes useful. However, most LISPs put function definitions
in a place other than the value cell. Some put them in a special place called
the *function cell*. These LISPs are the ones with a special function definition

access function like GETD. GETD retrieves the value of the function cell. There is a third place some LISPs put function definitions, which we shall discuss shortly. Meanwhile, notice that except for those LISPs that use the value cell for storing function definitions, the same function definition is used for a literal atom regardless of the environment we are in, and regardless of the number of times the value of the atom is bound. We say the function definition is associated with the atom *globally*—in every environment.

Besides the value cell and the function cell, there is one other structure associated with every literal atom. It is called the *property list*. A property list is a place where information of various sorts can be stored in association with a literal atom. Property lists are one of the unique features of LISP. Only literal atoms have property lists, not numbers, or other kinds of atoms. An atom's property list is associated with it globally; it has only one; it is the same in every environment; a change made to it in one environment changes it everywhere.

Conceptually, a property list is a collection of pairs. Each pair has a *property* (some call it an *indicator*), and a *value*. In most LISPs, the property must be an atom. In all LISPs, the value can be any S-expression. Often, the property list is an actual list, with the odd elements being the properties and the even ones being the values. Sometimes, though, a different method is used to represent property lists.

There are two main functions for dealing with property lists. The function for putting a pair onto a property list is PUT in some LISPs, and PUTPROP in others. The function always has three arguments. The first is invariably the atom whose property list is to be altered. The other two are the property and the value, but the order of these two varies among LISPs. I shall use the Franz LISP version, which is (PUTPROP atom value property), and from now on, whenever I say "PUTPROP" I will mean PUTPROP, or PUT, or whatever your LISP uses for this function. PUTPROP always is a SUBR, getting its three arguments evaluated. The value returned by PUTPROP also differs among LISPs, but since it is mainly used for its side-effect of changing the property list, we won't even discuss it. We might have a data base of people, each represented by the atom that is his or her first name. If we wanted to store John's age as 24, we could do (PUTPROP 'JOHN 24 'AGE).

The function for retrieving information from property lists is more consistent among LISPs. It invariably is (GET atom property), and it returns the value stored in that atom's property list under that property. So, to retrieve John's age, we would do (GET 'JOHN 'AGE). You might now realize that the third class of LISPs, in terms of where function definitions are stored, consists of those that store them on the property list of the atom, under the property that is the class of function it is. So,

if FN is an EXPR, the lambda form that is its definition is accessed by
(GET FN 'EXPR).

What if you try to GET a property value and it isn't there? For example,
what if we had not yet stored Mary's age and tried (GET 'MARY 'AGE)?
Usually, GET will return NIL in this case. Again, LISP's overuse of NIL
appears (NIL is an atom, the empty list, and LISP's representation of
FALSE). I said that a property value could be any S-expression, but if
you try to store NIL as the value of some property, that will be indistin-
guishable from not having stored any value with that property. Because
of this, some LISPs treat (PUTPROP atom NIL property) as
"remove property and its associated value from atom's property list". Some
LISPs have the special function (REMPROP atom property) to
do this.

If an atom, A, already has a value stored under some property, P, and
you do (PUTPROP 'A 'V 'P), the old value won't be modified, it
will be discarded, and V put in its place. So if you are keeping a list of
people's friends under the FRIENDS property, you should add Mary as
John's new friend by doing (PUTPROP 'JOHN (CONS 'MARY
(GET 'JOHN 'FRIENDS)) 'FRIENDS), not by (PUTPROP
'JOHN 'MARY 'FRIENDS), because then John will lose his old friends
when he takes up with Mary.

Exercises

1. Define X as (DE X (Y) (PRINT Y) (PRINT Y)). Define
   Y as (DE Y (X) (X X)). Evaluate (Y 'FOO). Does your
   LISP have global function definitions?

2. Define the function

   ```
   (DE FDEF (X)
       (DE YOUSAY (S)
           (PRINT (LIST 'YOU 'SAY S)))
       (YOUSAY X)).
   ```

   Evaluate (YOUSAY 'FIRST-TIME). Then, evaluate (FDEF
   'SECOND-TIME). Then, (YOUSAY 'THIRD-TIME). Is a
   function you define in one environment available in others?

3. What is your LISP's version of (PUTPROP atom value
   property)? Write it here:

   _____.

4. What is your LISP's version of (GET atom property)? Write
   it here:

   _____.

5. Does your LISP have a version of (REMPROP atom property)? If so, write it here:

   _____.

6. Record that John's age is 24 using JOHN's property list.

7. Retrieve John's age using GET.

8. See what you get if you now try to retrieve's Mary's age.

9. Franz LISP has a function (PLIST atom) that returns atom's whole property list. Does your LISP have such a function? If so, write it here: _____.

10. If your LISP has PLIST, do (PUTPROP 'JOHN NIL 'AGE) and then (PLIST 'JOHN), to see if storing a null value is equivalent to REMPROP.

11. Add Mary as John's new friend. Now add Jane as another. Use GET to make sure John has two friends. Now do (PUTPROP 'JOHN 'BILL 'FRIENDS). Has John lost his old friends?

12. Define a function (ADD-FRIEND PERSON FRIEND) so that whenever A is B's friend, B is also A's friend. Use it to give John, Mary, Jane, and Bill some friends. Now look at a friend list with GET. Is the property list a globally available structure?

13. Build a data base of 5–10 people. Store the list of people as the value of the property LIST under the atom PEOPLE. Give each person an age, some friends, and an occupation such as STUDENT, TEACHER, PROGRAMMER, etc. Writing functions as necessary, retrieve some information such as: all people who have an older friend; all people who are the youngest among their friends; all programmers under 15; all teachers under 30 who have at least one friend who is a student over 40.

Chapter 4

Where Now?

My hope is that you are now a good novice LISP programmer. You have experienced both pure, applicative LISP, and some non-applicative parts of LISP. Few, if any, experienced LISPers stick completely to the pure subset, but, if you are to make an informed choice, you must be used to both styles. I assumed that you might already have known some non-applicative languages, such as BASIC, FORTRAN, or Pascal. That is why I put off talking about non-applicative LISP until Section 3.1. Too often, I have seen people write "FORTRAN with parentheses," because they never gave pure LISP a chance.

Much of the discussion and many of the examples in this book have been about LISP itself. This is not because LISP has no applications, but because a major strength of LISP has always been the ability for programmers to create their own LISPish languages more suited to their applications than bare LISP. In fact, the dialects of LISP have grown out of collections of useful functions written at various installations, and used by the friends of the programmers. LISP can profitably be used for virtually any application any other programming language can be used for.

We have not discussed all of any major dialect of LISP. Some topics we left out, or barely discussed, are: compiling LISP, arrays, hunks, read-time macros, flavors, packages, dealing with exceptions, catch and throw. These were omitted because they are advanced topics, and because they are even less standardized across dialects than the topics we did discuss. You should make it a standard procedure to read through your manual regularly, or at least when you look one thing up to read several surrounding pages. You will then find new functions and capabilities you will immediately recognize a use for. You will also find new intriguing topics you will want to experiment with. After working through this book, you should be comfortable learning new LISP topics by experimentation.

There are several books that discuss more advanced topics in LISP programming than we got to. Most of these discuss using LISP for Artificial Intelligence, since that is where LISP has traditionally been most used. The following books include some introductory LISP, but at least half of each book is advanced LISP for Artificial Intelligence:

1. E. Charniak, C. K. Riesbeck, and D. V. McDermott. *Artificial Intelligence Programming*. Hillsdale, NJ: Lawrence Erlbaum, 1980.

2. R. C. Schank and C. K. Riesbeck. *Inside Computer Understanding*. Hillsdale, NJ: Lawrence Erlbaum, 1981.

3. P. H. Winston and B. K. P. Horn. *LISP*. Reading, MA: Addison-Wesley, 1981.

4. P. H. Winston and B. K. P. Horn. *LISP, 2nd ed*. Reading, MA: Addison-Wesley, 1984.

The following books are solely advanced LISP for Artificial Intelligence. In fact, the book you are reading was written as a "prequel."

1. S. C. Shapiro. *Techniques of Artificial Intelligence*. New York: D. Van Nostrand, 1979.

2. S. C. Shapiro. *Techniques of Artificial Intelligence, 2nd ed*. Belmont, CA: Wadsworth, forthcoming.

The following book is a formal introduction to LISP in the setting of abstract data types and programming languages. It will give you more of an idea of how LISP can be implemented.

J. R. Allen. *Anatomy of LISP*. New York: McGraw-Hill, 1978.

Of course, the only way to improve your LISP ability is to use it. Even if you ultimately translate a program into another language, LISP is excellent for initial design and test, what has become known as "fast prototyping." Versions of LISP are spreading to all operating systems, and all computers, including personal computers and LISP machines—computers for which LISP is the native language. You may well find that LISP is the only programming language you will need.

PERSONALIZED MANUAL

Fill in the lines below to create a personalized manual for your reference. The page numbers shown indicate where you should have first discovered and noted the information. If your LISP does not have the feature listed, write "None," or some other similar notation.

Dialect of LISP _____

Computer _____

Operating System _____

Terminal _____

Table of Contents

1. Changing Environments
2. Typing to LISP
3. Numerical Functions
4. Numerical Predicate Functions
5. Equality Predicates
6. Other Predicate Functions
7. List Synthesis Functions
8. List Analysis Functions
9. Miscellaneous Functions
10. Control Functions
11. Function-Defining Functions
12. Dealing with Files
13. Functions for Debugging and Testing
14. Editing
15. Evaluation Functions
16. Input/Output Functions
17. Property List Functions
18. Destructive List Manipulation Functions

1. Changing Environments
Procedure for getting into LISP (page 2)

_____

_____

Procedure for getting out of LISP (pages 2, 3)

_____

_____

Command to enter Break-level (pages 3, 45) _____
Command to leave Break-level, continuing computation (pages 3, 45)

Command to leave Break-level, aborting computation (pages 3, 45)

_____

2. Typing to LISP
Top-level LISP prompt (page 3) _____
Break-level LISP prompt (page 3) _____

Upper/lower case preference (page 3) _____

EVAL vs. EVALQUOTE at top-level (pages 117, 118) _____

Backspace character (page 5) _____

Line erase character (page 5) _____

List erase character (page 10) _____

Interrupt key (pages 3, 45) _____

Comment character (page 5) _____

Escape character (page 7) _____

Escape brackets (page 7) _____

Quote character (page 6) _____

String delimiters (page 7) _____

Backquote character, comma and at sign features (page 91) _____

3. Numerical Functions

Addition (page 12) _____

Subtraction (pages 14–16) _____

Multiplication (pages 14–16) _____

Division (pages 14–16) _____

Unary minus (pages 14–16) _____

Absolute value (page 39) _____

Square root (pages 14–16) _____

4. Numerical Predicate Functions

NUMBERP (page 36) _____

FIXP (page 36) _____

FLOATP (page 36) _____

ZEROP (page 36) _____

MINUSP (page 36) _____

PLUSP (page 36) _____

GREATERP (page 36) _____

LESSP (page 37) _____

5. Equality Predicates

Equality of literal atoms (page 36) _____

Equality of fixed-point numbers (page 36) _____

Equality of floating-point numbers (page 62) _____

Equality of any numbers (page 62) _____

Equality of strings (page 62) _____

Equality of S-expressions (page 62) _____

6. Other Predicate Functions

ATOM (page 36) _____

NULL (page 36) _____

LISTP (page 36) _____

AND (page 36) _____

OR (page 37) _____

NOT (page 36) _____

Print name compare (page 75) _____

7. List Synthesis Functions
CONS (page 17) ———————————————————
LIST (page 74) ————————————————————
COPY (page 55) ———————————————————
APPEND (page 55) ————————————————
Substitute all top-level occurrences (page 56) ———————
List of all arguments of nospread function (page 74) ———

8. List Analysis Functions
CAR (page 17) ————————————————————
CDR (page 17) ————————————————————
CxyzR (page 18) ————————————————
LENGTH (page 50) ————————————————
MEMBER (page 50) ————————————————

9. Miscellaneous Functions
SET (pages 97, 99) ————————————————
SETQ (pages 97, 99) ——————————————
Nth argument of nospread function (page 74) ——————

10. Control Functions
COND (pages 37–39, 101) ———————————
IF (page 74) ——————————————————————
LET (page 105) ———————————————————
LET* (page 105) ———————————————————
Map function over list of arguments, giving list of results (pages 77, 81)
————————————————————————
Map function over list of arguments for side-effect (page 116)
————————————————————————
Map function over list of arguments, and NCONC list of results (page 129)
————————————————————————
PROG (page 110) ———————————————————
    Textually non-enclosed RETURN allowed? (page 111) ———
    Textually non-enclosed GO allowed? (page 111) ———
PROGN (page 101) ————————————————
PROG1 (page 101) ————————————————
PROG2 (page 101) ————————————————
Structured Loop (page 123) ————————————
————————————————————————
————————————————————————
————————————————————————

11. Function-Defining Functions
To define an EXPR (pages 23, 70, 71, 101) ————————
To define an EXPR* (pages 70, 71, 101) ————————
    List/number of arguments method for EXPR*s (pages 70, 71) ———
To define an FEXPR (pages 70, 71, 101) ————————

To define an FEXPR* (pages 70, 71, 87, 101) _____
        List/number of arguments method for FEXPR*s (pages 70, 71) _____
To define a nospread macro (pages 88, 91, 101) _____
To define a spread macro (pages 90, 92, 101) _____
Definition access function (page 26) _____
Pretty-printing a function (page 26) _____

12. Dealing with Files
LISP file vs. text file method (page 31) _____
To create a file (page 31) _____
To store functions in a file (page 31) _____
To load functions from a file (page 31) _____
To comment a function on a file (pages 31, 32) _____
To list a file on the screen (page 31) _____
To print a file on a printer (page 32) _____

13. Functions for Debugging and Testing
TRACE (page 24) _____
UNTRACE (page 24) _____
MACROEXPAND (page 91) _____
Call the garbage collector (page 131) _____
Turn on/off garbage collection reporting (page 131) _____
Seeing stack of function calls (page 46) _____
Timing the execution of a form (pages 50, 111) _____

14. Editing
Begin editing (page 40) _____
Terminate editing (page 41) _____
Print the S-expression (page 40) _____
Change to sub-list (page 40) _____
Add an S-expression (page 41) _____
Delete an S-expression (page 41) _____
Replace an S-expression (page 41) _____
Remove a pair of parentheses (page 41) _____
Enclose some S-expressions in parentheses (page 41) _____

15. Evaluation Functions
EVAL (pages 67, 87) _____
APPLY (page 81) _____
FUNCALL (page 131) _____
QUOTE (page 18–19) _____
Closure producer (page 87) _____

16. Input/Output Functions
PRINT (pages 115, 116) _____
Print carriage return, new line (page 116) _____
Print without escape characters (page 116) _____
READ (page 117) _____

17. Property List Functions
PUT or PUTPROP (page 134) ————————————————————
GET (page 134) ————————————————————————————
REMPROP (page 135) —————————————————————————
PLIST (page 135) ————————————————————————————

18. Destructive List Manipulation Functions
RPLACA (page 130) —————————————————————————
RPLACD (page 130) —————————————————————————
NCONC (page 130) ——————————————————————————
Map function over list of arguments, and NCONC list of results (page 129)
——

Others (page 62) ————————————————————————————
——
——
——

INDEX